SPORTS CARS

SPORTS CARS

HIGH-PERFORMANCE MACHINES

GENERAL EDITOR: CRAIG CHEETHAM

Grange
BOOKS

This edition first published in 2003 for Grange Books
An imprint of Grange Books plc
The Grange
Kingsnorth Industrial Estate
Hoo, nr Rochester
Kent ME3 9ND
www.grangebooks.co.uk

A catalogue record for this book is available from the British Library.

ISBN 1-84013-581-6

Produced by
Amber Books Ltd
Bradley's Close
74–77 White Lion Street
London N1 9PF
www.amberbooks.co.uk

Printed in Italy

This material was previously published as part of the reference set *Hot Cars*

CONTENTS

Introduction   6

Alfa Romeo   8
Aston Martin   16
Austin Healey   24
BMW   28
Bugatti   36
Chevrolet   40
Datsun   48
De Tomaso   52
DeLorean   56
Dodge   60
Ferrari   64
Ford   84
Honda   92
Jaguar   96
Lamborghini   104
Lancia   116
Light Car Company   120
Lotus   124
Maserati   132
Mazda   136
McLaren   144
Mercedes   148
MG   152
Panoz   156
Porsche   160
Renault   176
Toyota   180
TVR   188

Index   192

Introduction

Defining a sports car is a difficult task—to anyone with a drop of petrol running through their veins, selecting the 46 cars featured in this book would be an arduous and confusing task.

Indeed, it was. There are literally hundreds of performance vehicles from around the globe that could rightly claim to be called sports cars, but we feel that the varied and international collection we have here represents everything a sports car stands for.

That means each car had to satisfy a number of painstaking criteria. In each case, it had to have been designed for a specific purpose and not merely derived from a humdrum compact saloon or hatchback. Each car had to be aspirational enough to make your neighbours jealous, yet that didn't mean it had to be priceless or exotic. Indeed, the very nature of a sports car defines that it should have a degree of practicality. It should also have style—let's face it, great looks are enough to make a car instantly desirable

whatever its engine or roadholding capabilities. But great looks aren't enough to earn a car a place in this book—every vehicle within these pages offers much more. By definition, a sports car must be sporting to drive, and that means it must have either blistering performance or tactile handling. Most of the cars in this book have both.

The machines featured here have much in common. They're all true greats—the best of their kind. Each one is a thoroughbred of the traditional sports car lineage that can trace its roots back to the original veteran racing cars of the turn of the century.

Of course, modern technology, improved engine design and elevated levels of passenger comfort mean the sports cars of today vary strongly from those of yesteryear—but the manufacturers who build these cars know that

The flowing lines and elongated hood of the E-type Jaguar were a revelation when it was unveiled in 1961.

The Lamborghini Countach redefined the sports car in the 1980s with its outrageous styling and remarkable acceleration.

they mustn't make them too soft.

While some sports cars are user-friendly, and some brutal and demanding to drive, every car featured in this book has been chosen because it rewards the enthusiastic driver. There's not a car in here that's uninspiring to drive—every single one of them has been built around the driver to offer the sharpest handling, breathtaking acceleration and jaw-dropping design that have the ability to inject a healthy dose of fun into everyday motoring.

Each offers a unique blend of performance, desirability and stunning styling that earns it its place among the elite, and we hope that as you cast your eyes over these pages you'll agree we've chosen some of the finest machinery offered over the past 40 years.

Yet we've kept our feet firmly on the ground. Although this book features some of the legendary performance cars that many of us aspire to but few can afford, such as the Lamborghini Diablo, Porsche 959 and Ferrari 355, it also includes a number of motors that have always offered less wealthy owners the chance to take a step onto the sports car ladder.

Cars like the MGB, Mazda MX-5 Miata and Toyota MR2 are all celebrated here, as they rub shoulders with the exotica most of us can only

dream of. And in terms of driver pleasure and performance, even in such strong company they don't get left behind.

The aim of this book is to put you behind the wheel. To give you, the reader, the opportunity to experience them up close and personal. With stunning detail photography and expert driving impressions, this isn't just a collection of notes about a random selection of cars. It practically allows you to hear the engines roar and smell the burning rubber as they charge through your imagination.

With in-depth technological specifications, close-up detail pictures and an overview of the history of each car, our aim is to offer you extensive and detailed trivia about some of the world's finest drivers' cars, to give you an expert insight into some of the best cars the world has to offer and to inspire you into maybe enjoying one for yourself.

So sit back, fasten your safety belt and enter the world of the greatest sports cars ever built— whether you're poring over a Lamborghini Miura or an Austin-Healey 3000, you're in for the ride of your life…

Alfa Romeo **SPIDER**

While other manufacturers have looked back with retro design for their sports cars, Alfa Romeo has looked forward. The new Spider looks like no other, and is as striking and modern as a motor-show concept car but with all the traditional Alfa virtues that the enthusiast demands.

"...all about style and class."

"The Spider is all about style and class. You feel good just being in this Alfa, knowing other drivers would rather be in your car. On a smooth road, the Spider is as impressive as it looks—the new multi-link suspension works perfectly. The car flows through corners at high speeds with the twin-spark, twin-cam engine eagerly singing to 7,000 rpm—and even then it's hard to tell the Alfa is front-wheel drive. It's true that the Spider suffers from cowl shake, but Alfa knows its customers will forgive it."

The leather-trimmed cockpit is comfortable and well-appointed.

Milestones

1989 The Geneva Motor Show sees the debut of the prototype Alfa SZ. It first appears as a coupe and later as a convertible and uses Alfa Romeo Alfetta running gear. Although it looks quite different from the current Spider, the design influences are clear.

The SZ brought Alfa back into the sports car market.

1991 The Proteo concept car appears at the Geneva Motor Show. It is based on Alfa's large sedan, the 164, and uses the 164's V6 engine, but tuned to produce 260 bhp. Proteo has both four-wheel drive and four-wheel steer. Although neither the 4WD or 4WS is carried over into the present Spider, the body styling clearly inspired the current car.

1994 Alfa unveils the Spider a year before anyone can buy one.

The handsome GTV has all the Spider's style, but with a roof.

1995 Alfa's new Spider goes on sale in June.

UNDER THE SKIN

Front-wheel drive

Alfa Romeo's first front-wheel drive convertible sports car has the engine mounted transversely. It also breaks with tradition by having a modern suspension system with struts at the front and a multi-link suspension system at the rear, instead of the previous double wishbones at the front and coil-sprung live rear axle.

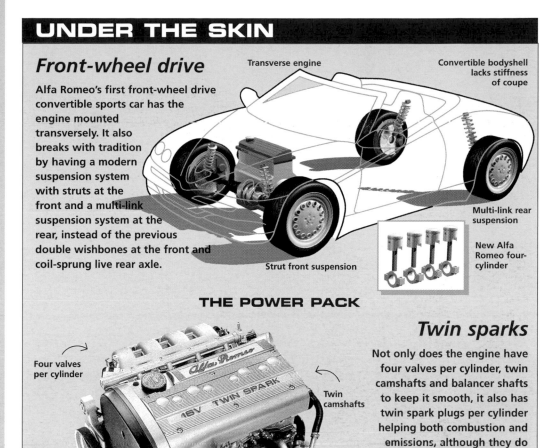

Transverse engine

Convertible bodyshell lacks stiffness of coupe

Multi-link rear suspension

New Alfa Romeo four-cylinder

Strut front suspension

THE POWER PACK

Four valves per cylinder

Twin camshafts

Belt drive for ancillaries and camshafts

Basic engine designed by Fiat

Balancer shafts reduce vibration

Twin sparks

Not only does the engine have four valves per cylinder, twin camshafts and balancer shafts to keep it smooth, it also has twin spark plugs per cylinder helping both combustion and emissions, although they do little to increase the power: Some rival 2-liter engines are more powerful. The basic engine design is Fiat's, but Alfa was responsible for the design of the twin-spark cylinder head— an established Alfa Romeo feature, seen on sedans like the 75 and 164.

More power

Although the four-cylinder model will account for most sales, the 3-liter 24-valve V6 GTV coupe offers the greater performance that the car deserves. It has 220 bhp and 198 lb-ft of torque, enough to give it an impressive 0-60 mph time of 6.7 seconds and a top speed of 149 mph.

If you want Alfa V6 performance, you'll have to order a GTV.

Alfa Romeo SPIDER

There's always been a convertible Spider sports car in Alfa's model line, but never before has it been front-wheel drive. Alfa has managed the change perfectly—the new car delivers all the enthusiast expects.

Strut front suspension

Sports cars like Alfas traditionally had double wishbone front suspension, but the Spider shows the same results can be achieved with simpler struts.

Tiny convertible top

The upswept rear lines of the Spider mean the convertible top is actually very small.

Transverse engine

The Spider is the first Alfa sports car to have the engine mounted transversely.

Twin-spark

Naturally, the Alfa has a twin-cam engine with two spark plugs for each cylinder, an approach Alfa used in some of its racing cars in the 1960s.

Anti-lock brakes

ABS is standard and works in conjunction with four-wheel disc brakes. Larger Brembo units are fitted to the more powerful and heavier V6 version of the mechanically similar GTV.

Leather trimmed

The Alfa is a luxury convertible as well as a sports car, and the interior and seats are leather trimmed.

Rigid top cover

The Spider's looks would have been spoiled with an untidy top staked behind the seats, so it's hidden away under a rigid panel.

Rear light strip

Like the Fiat Coupe, the Spider has a high rear end, but the rear light strip right across the back of the car minimizes the effect.

Multi-link rear suspension

The Spider's multi-link system gives precise wheel control, good handling and a good ride.

Specifications

1997 Alfa Romeo Spider

ENGINE

Type: In-line four cylinder
Construction: Iron block, alloy head
Valve gear: Four valves per cylinder operated by twin overhead camshafts
Bore and stroke: 3.27 in. x 3.58 in.
Displacement: 1,970 cc
Compression ratio: 9.5:1
Induction system: Electronic fuel injection
Maximum power: 150 bhp at 6,200 rpm
Maximum torque: 137 lb-ft at 4,000 rpm

TRANSMISSION

Five-speed manual

BODY/CHASSIS

Unitary steel construction with two-door, two-seat convertible body

SPECIAL FEATURES

Sculpted Alfa Romeo grill is a styling feature that first appeared on the series-topping 164 sedan.

The four small headlights are actually a styling trick. There are two large lights shining through four small holes.

RUNNING GEAR

Steering: Rack-and-pinion
Front suspension: MacPherson struts with lower wishbones and anti-roll bar
Rear suspension: Multi-link with coil springs, telescopic shocks and anti-roll bar
Brakes: Vented discs front, solid discs rear, 10.1 in. dia. (front), 9.5 in. dia. (rear)
Wheels: Alloy 6 in. x 15 in.
Tires: 195/760 ZR15

DIMENSIONS

Length: 168.7 in.   **Width:** 70 in.
Height: 51.7 in.   **Wheelbase:** 100 in.
Track: 59 in. (front), 159.3 in. (rear)
Weight: 3,021 lbs.

Alfa Romeo GIULIETTA SZ

The SZ is an aluminum Zagato-bodied short-chassis version of Alfa Romeo's Giulietta coupe. By reducing weight and increasing power, Alfa created a lithe and delicate coupe that was highly competitive in the 1,300-cc race and rally classes in the early 1960s.

"...smoothness and precision."

"The inside of the SZ is basic, with just a couple of hip-hugging bucket seats and a cluster of instruments. The sliding windows are Plexiglass and so there is plenty of wind noise at speed. But it is the engine that dominates—its smooth, low revving warble changes to a high-pitched scream as it reaches the redline. The Alfa has informative steering but with a nervous feel; the SZ rewards the driver with smooth and precise driving."

Built for competition, the SZ is a driving enthusiast's delight.

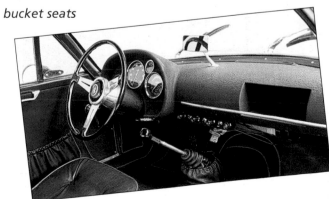

Milestones

1956 Zagato unofficially
re-bodies the crashed Giulietta SV belonging to Carlo and Dore Leto di Priolo. The car is 238 lbs. lighter and is immediately very competitive. Approximately 18 cars are built from 1957 to 1959.

The Alfa Romeo SS was designed and built by Bertone.

1959 Alfa Romeo signs
a deal to supply chassis platforms and engines to Zagato.

1960 The official SZ,
with a shorter wheelbase and fitted with a 100-bhp engine from the Giulietta SS, is launched at the Geneva show.

The SZ name was reborn in the late 1980s in this exotic form.

1962 The SZ becomes
the SZT with a new aerodynamic Kamm-style tail.

1963 SZ production
ends. In all, 169 round and 44 square-tail cars have been built.

UNDER THE SKIN

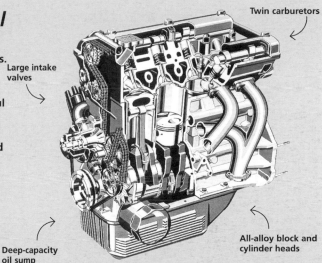

Live rear axle

Wishbone front suspension

Coil springs all around

All-alloy in-line four

Few changes

The basic engineering of the Giulietta was so good that few changes were needed to make the shorter and lighter SZ into a winner. Alfa fine-tuned the components to near-perfection. Coil springs and wishbones are fitted up front, and the rigid rear axle—sprung by coils and located by an 'A' frame—gives excellent handling.

THE POWER PACK

Light and powerful

Alfa built its reputation on twin-cam engines in the 1920s and 1930s. The Giulietta's all-alloy 1,290-cc in-line four is attractive with its polished cam covers and a beautiful finned alloy oil pan. Large valves and twin Weber carburetors allow the engine to breath efficiently and to rev freely and sweetly. It is also very tuneable: Virgilio Conrero of Turin, the acknowledged master of Alfa engines, was able to increase the engine's power to 127 bhp, producing a top speed of 130 mph in the slippery SZ.

Twin carburetors

Large intake valves

Deep-capacity oil sump

All-alloy block and cylinder heads

First of the few

Zagato, traditionally the most radical of the Italian coachbuilders, forged strong links with Alfa Romeo after the SZ. During the 1960s and 1970s it built several other production models using Alfa components. One of the most unusual of them all was the 1989 SZ.

The SZ started the relationship between Alfa and Zagato.

Alfa Romeo GIULIETTA SZ

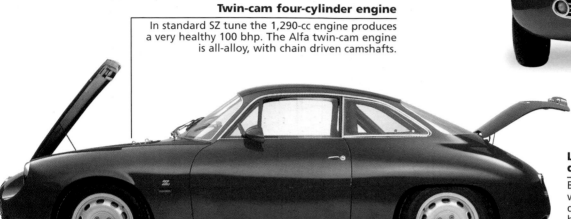

The SZ was the ultimate car in the Giulietta range. Its combination of speed, lightness, agility, and stamina made it a fine competition car as well as highly satisfying to drive on the open road.

Twin-cam four-cylinder engine

In standard SZ tune the 1,290-cc engine produces a very healthy 100 bhp. The Alfa twin-cam engine is all-alloy, with chain driven camshafts.

Large alloy drum brakes

Before disc brakes became widely available, the SZ's drums were among the best you could find on any production car. They used triple shoes on later models but never required servo assistance because the SZ is so light.

Short wheelbase

By shortening the Giulietta's wheelbase by 5.1 inches, Alfa made the SZ lighter and more agile. However, compared to the Sprint and the Spider it has a choppier ride and wet weather handling can be tricky.

Rounded tail design

Most SZs have this neat, rounded rear end, but the last 44 cars have a squared-off Kamm-style tail designed to reduce turbulence.

Five-speed transmission

Only the most expensive exotic cars had five speeds in the 1950s and early 1960s— electric overdrive was much more common. The all-synchromesh Alfa Romeo transmission has a fine action and the ratios are perfectly spaced to make the best of the engine's power band.

Sliding Perspex windows

Lightweight, with no bulky mechanism inside the door, and quicker to operate, these sliding Plexiglass windows were ideal for a car like the SZ, which was primarily intended for competition use.

Specifications

1960 Alfa Romeo Giulietta SZ

ENGINE

Type: In-line four-cylinder

Construction: Alloy cylinder block and head

Valve gear: Two valves per cylinder operated by chain-driven double overhead camshafts

Bore and stroke: 2.91 in. x 2.95 in.

Displacement: 1,290 cc

Compression ratio: 9:1

Induction system: Two twin-choke Weber carburetors

Maximum power: 100 bhp at 6,000 rpm

Maximum torque: 80 lb-ft at 4,500 rpm

TRANSMISSION

Five-speed manual

BODY/CHASSIS

Aluminum body on steel platform chassis

SPECIAL FEATURES

Stylish retaining pins keep the hood in place at high speeds.

Early SZs have exposed headlights, while later examples are fitted with flush-mounted headlight covers.

RUNNING GEAR

Steering: Worm-and-nut

Front suspension: Wishbones and coil springs

Rear suspension: Live axle with coil springs and trailing arms

Brakes: Finned alloy drums, 10.5-in. dia. (front), 10-in. dia. (rear)

Wheels: Borrani alloy rim, steel center, 15-in. dia.

Tires: Pirelli Cinturato 155-15

DIMENSIONS

Length: 151.5 in. **Width:** 60.5 in.

Height: 48.5 in. **Wheelbase:** 88.6 in.

Track: 50.8 in. (front and rear)

Weight: 1,890 lbs.

Aston Martin **DB7**

With Ford's money behind the company, Aston Martin was at last able to build a worthy successor to the DB5 and DB6 of the 1960s, fast and beautiful in the true Aston tradition.

"Supercharged sophistication."

"You soon see why the Aston is so expensive; the chassis is simply wonderful, enabling the DB7 to tackle tight corners, sweeping curves, off camber bends—it's all the same to the Aston and it does it with the same finesse as a Jaguar. It's got enough power to push the back end out, but it does it in a very controlled way. And thanks to powerful brakes and the instant power that the super-charger makes available, the Aston's combination is perfect."

The modern and stylish interior is comfortable as well as functional.

Milestones

1965 Last of the numbered DB series, the DB6, appears, named after Aston Martin owner David Brown. The DB6's successor, the DBS, uses a V8 engine, ending the six-cylinder line until the current car appears.

The sporty DB7 is the spiritual successor to the famous DB6 of the 1960s.

1992 Aston Martin Oxford Ltd. is formed to produce a new Aston Martin. Mechanically, it is closely related to the Jaguar XJS because now Aston Martin and Jaguar are both part of Ford.

The DB7 was originally for Jaguar, and at the last hour was used for Aston Martin.

1994 The DB7 makes its debut.

1996 Two more years of development results in the DB7 Volante model with its power convertible top, intended primarily for the U.S. market.

UNDER THE SKIN

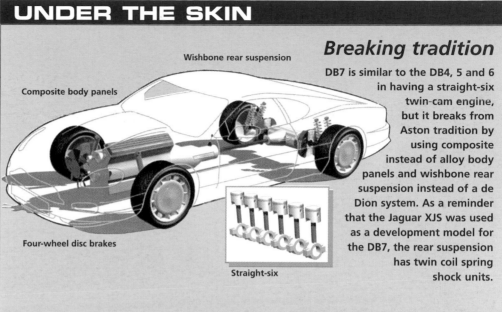

Composite body panels

Wishbone rear suspension

Four-wheel disc brakes

Straight-six

Breaking tradition

DB7 is similar to the DB4, 5 and 6 in having a straight-six twin-cam engine, but it breaks from Aston tradition by using composite instead of alloy body panels and wishbone rear suspension instead of a de Dion system. As a reminder that the Jaguar XJS was used as a development model for the DB7, the rear suspension has twin coil spring shock units.

THE POWER PACK

Supercharged six

Thanks to its mechanically driven Eaton supercharger, the 3.2-liter all-alloy straight-six, twin-cam 24-valve engine, developed with the help of TWR, produces more than 100 bhp per liter, the sign of a true high-performance engine. The supercharger also helps to give a vast amount of low-down torque as well as outright power and the maximum torque is produced at only 3,000 rpm.

Twin camshafts

Four valves per cylinder

Alloy block and heads

Eaton supercharger

Chop top

Two years after the DB7 first appeared, Aston Martin introduced the Volante convertible model. It's a bit heavier and slower and has softer, more compliant, suspension, but the attraction of top-down supercar motoring overcomes the drawbacks.

Volante is the traditional name Aston Martin gives to its convertible models.

Aston Martin DB7

With the DB7, Aston Martin discarded the brutal appearance of its V8 range in favor of a smooth, sleek look designed in Britain. Its beauty did not hide the fact it was a seriously fast car, though.

Straight-six engine

The DB7's short-stroke engine is an in-line six-cylinder with four valves per cylinder. At 3,239 cc it's smaller but more powerful than any of the straight-six twin cams used in the previous DB range.

Fiberglass bodywork

The DB7 would be even heavier if it had conventional steel body panels. The fiberglass bodywork is lighter than steel and also cheaper to produce than the hand-finished alloy panels of traditional Aston Martins.

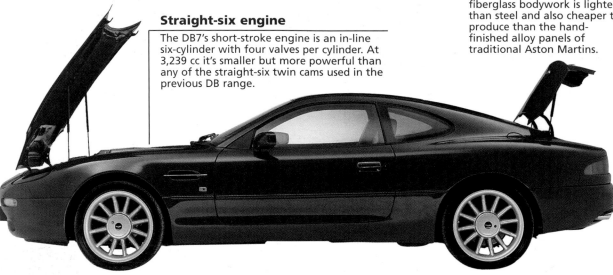

Same wheelbase as DB6

Curiously enough, the DB7 has exactly the same wheelbase as the old DB6, although the body is wider and longer and has a significantly wider track.

Outstanding brakes

Although only the front discs are vented, the DB7's brakes are absolutely outstanding and can stop the heavy car from 60 mph in only 2.8 seconds.

Leather interior

An Aston Martin wouldn't be an Aston Martin without a luxurious interior and the DB7 features Connolly hide. It is available in bright two-tone finishes where the DBs of the 1960s were more restrained and less stylish.

Front-heavy weight distribution

Although the engine is all alloy, engine accessories like the supercharger and intercooler help tip the DB7's weight toward the front, giving a 54/46 front-to-rear distribution.

2+2 accommodation

Two rear passengers can just about be crammed into the upright rear seats with their very narrow seat bottoms, making the DB7 a 2+2.

Intercooler

Forced induction heats the intake air and thins it so an intercooler is fitted to the supercharger, just as it is with a turbocharger, to cool the air before it reaches the engine, restoring its density and increasing the power the engine can produce.

Specifications
1997 Aston Martin DB7

ENGINE

Type: In-line six-cylinder
Construction: Alloy block and head
Valve gear: Four valves per cylinder operated by twin overhead camshafts
Bore and stroke: 3.58 in. x 3.26 in.
Displacement: 3,239 cc
Compression ratio: 8.3:1
Induction system: Electronic sequential fuel injection with Eaton mechanical supercharger and intercooler
Maximum power: 335 bhp at 5,750 rpm
Maximum torque: 400 lb-ft at 3,000 rpm

TRANSMISSION

Five-speed manual

BODY/CHASSIS

Steel floorpan with fiberglass 2+2 coupe body

SPECIAL FEATURES

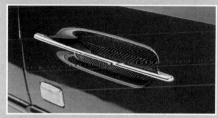

Vents behind the front wheel arches are similar to the 1960s DB4, 5 and 6s.

A true 2+2, the DB7 has separate, small bucket seats for rear passengers.

RUNNING GEAR

Steering: Rack-and-pinion
Front suspension: Double wishbones, coil springs, telescopic shocks and anti-roll bar
Rear suspension: Double wishbones, coil springs, telescopic shocks and anti-roll bar
Brakes: Four-wheel discs, vented, 13.2 in. dia. (front), solid 12 in. dia. (rear); ABS
Wheels: Alloy, 8 in. x 18 in.
Tires: 245/40 ZR18

DIMENSIONS

Length: 182.3 in.   **Width:** 71.6 in.
Height: 49.8 in.   **Wheelbase:** 102 in.
Track: 60 in. (front), 59.8 in. (rear)
Weight: 3,858 lbs.

Aston Martin VANTAGE

Adding twin superchargers turned the Virage into one of the fastest luxury coupes in the world, with a top speed of 190 mph. For the new coupe, Aston Martin chose to revive the old Vantage name.

"...requires a daring driver."

"Take time to adjust to the luxurious interior. The big V8 engine is loud though slightly muffled by the well insulated cabin. It quickly becomes evident that this car is different from all the others. It can reach 100 mph in 10 seconds. Flog the Vantage around a test track and you can extract a shocking 190 mph out of it, but it requires a daring driver with a firm hand. Understeer is detectable because of the car's massive torque output."

Connolly leather and a walnut trimmed dash: this could only be an Aston Martin.

Milestones

1988 Aston Martin's first new

car in 20 years, the Virage, makes its debut at the British Motor Show in Birmingham. It's an instant success with many orders taken. Production begins in 1989.

A new V8 engine gave the Aston Martin the performance and image that it desperately needed.

1990 A Volante convertible joins the

standard Virage coupe, followed by a Shooting Brake wagon and two Lagonda four-door models.

The most unusual Virage model is the Lagonda Shooting Brake.

1993 The standard Virage gets a new four-

speed automatic transmission. After experimenting with a 6.3-liter version of the V8, Aston decides on a supercharged prototype of the smaller 5.3-liter quad-cam V8 engine. Its new performance mode becomes known as the Vantage which boasts suspension and body modifications.

UNDER THE SKIN

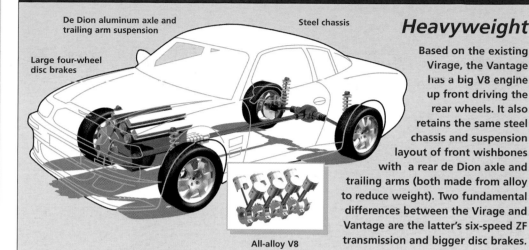

De Dion aluminum axle and trailing arm suspension

Steel chassis

Large four-wheel disc brakes

All-alloy V8

Heavyweight

Based on the existing Virage, the Vantage has a big V8 engine up front driving the rear wheels. It also retains the same steel chassis and suspension layout of front wishbones with a rear de Dion axle and trailing arms (both made from alloy to reduce weight). Two fundamental differences between the Virage and Vantage are the latter's six-speed ZF transmission and bigger disc brakes.

THE POWER PACK

Supercharged

In the late 1980s, Aston Martin asked Corvette tuning expert Reeves Callaway to rework the cylinder heads on the Aston four-cam V8 for installation into the new Virage. This helped to produce an impressive 330 bhp. Three years later, the compression ratio for the Vantage was lowered to enable the use of twin Eaton mechanically-driven intercooled superchargers, running at 10 psi. This increased output to 550 bhp and an incredible 550 lb-ft of torque.

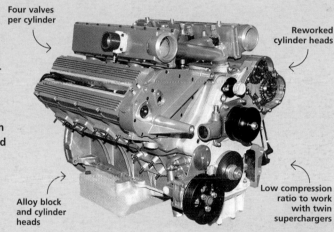

Four valves per cylinder

Reworked cylinder heads

Alloy block and cylinder heads

Low compression ratio to work with twin superchargers

P977 RVS

Britain's best

Although now owned by Ford, Aston Martin continues to go its own way. The Vantage is a true gentleman's supercar, capable of embarrassing Italian exotics, yet is still able to seat four in comfort and be used for daily driving chores.

As well as being fast, the Vantage has a practical side too.

Aston Martin VANTAGE

The Vantage is the most uncompromising car Aston Martin has ever built. Designed for brute power and stunning outright performance, no expense is spared. It's quite expensive yet exceptionally powerful.

Twin superchargers

Plenty of power and unbelievable torque is achieved by using dual Eaton superchargers.

Quad-cam V8

Modifications to Aston Martin's long-established V8 engine gave it new cylinder heads, which improved power, torque, emissions and gas mileage.

Six-speed transmission

Like the Virage from which it was developed, the Vantage has a German ZF manual transmission, but with six forward speeds.

Massive brakes

Despite the alloy body and V8 engine, the Vantage is a real heavyweight and requires huge brakes—the front discs measure 14 inches across. ABS is standard.

Alloy bodywork

Hand-crafted alloy bodywork is a hallmark of Aston Martin cars, and, not surprisingly, the Vantage continues this tradition. None of the bodywork is load-bearing and so structural strength is not an issue.

De Dion axle

Both the Virage and Vantage have a unique cast-alloy de Dion axle. It is well located using Watt linkage to prevent sideways movement of the axle.

Specifications

1994 Aston Martin Vantage

ENGINE

Type: V8

Construction: Alloy block and heads

Valve gear: Four valves per cylinder operated by twin overhead camshafts per bank of cylinders

Bore and stroke: 3.94 in. x 3.35 in.

Displacement: 5,340 cc

Compression ratio: 8.2:1

Induction system: Electronic fuel injection with twin Eaton superchargers

Maximum power: 550 bhp at 6,500 rpm

Maximum torque: 550 lb-ft at 4,000 rpm

TRANSMISSION

ZF six-speed manual

BODY/CHASSIS

Steel skeleton with alloy panels forming two-door 2+2 coupe

SPECIAL FEATURES

Triple headlights are a unique feature of the Vantage.

Twin superchargers on the V8 engine produce a massive amount of torque.

RUNNING GEAR

Steering: Rack-and-pinion

Front suspension: Double wishbones with coil springs, telescopic shock absorbers and anti-roll bar

Rear suspension: Cast-alloy de Dion axle with trailing arms, Watt linkage, coil springs and telescopic shock absorbers

Brakes: Vented discs, 14-in. dia. (front), 12.2-in. dia. (rear)

Wheels: Alloy, 10 x 18 in.

Tires: 285/45 ZR18

DIMENSIONS

Length: 186.8 in. **Width:** 76.5 in.

Height: 52.0 in. **Wheelbase:** 102.8 in.

Track: 60.9 in. (front), 61.7 in. (rear)

Weight: 4,230 lbs.

Austin-Healey 3000

The combination of Austin's 3-liter engine and Donald Healey's sports car produced a rugged classic with enormous character and an impressive competition record.

"...it needs a firm hand."

"Healeys are not the easiest of cars to drive, as the 'works' rally drivers would testify. Steering is heavy and shifting is awkward (although flicking a switch in and out of overdrive is delightfully easy). The Healey's basic tendency is to go straight at corners, so it needs a firm hand. Bumpy roads will throw the stiffly sprung back axle off line, make the scuttle shake and the steering wheel kick. Apply too much power in corners and you easily trade understeer for oversteer, though that's just an accepted part of the car's character."

MkIII Austin-Healey 3000 has improved interior with a wooden dashboard.

Milestones

1952 Healey 100 is completed in time for the British Motor Show. It has a four-cylinder, 90-bhp Austin A90 engine. The design is built by BMC as an Austin-Healey.

1956 100 turns into the 100/6 when equipped with Austin's 2.6-liter, six-cylinder engine.

The 3000 was a great rally car. The fiercest of all 'works' cars were Mark IIIs with 210 bhp.

1959 3000 introduced with power up to 124 bhp.

1960 Proving what a great rally car the 3000 is, Pat Moss wins the Liege-Rome-Liege Rally.

1961 Power increases to 132 bhp producing the 3000 MkII. A restyle takes place in the following year.

Austin-Healey experimented with a closed version of the 3000, but it never reached production.

1964 Definitive 3000, the MkIII appears. Rauno Aaltonen/Tony Ambrose win the Spa-Sofia-Liege rally in one.

UNDER THE SKIN

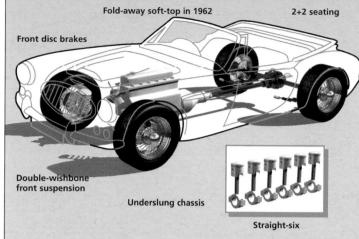

Fold-away soft-top in 1962
2+2 seating
Front disc brakes
Double-wishbone front suspension
Underslung chassis
Straight-six

Limited travel

A traditional ladder-frame chassis is used with a cruciform brace, but where such chassis usually kick up at the rear to clear the axle, the Healey's chassis rails run below, limiting suspension travel. Front suspension is a modified form of that used on the A90 sedan, while cam-and-peg steering is used. Earlier Healeys have brake drums all around but the 3000 uses discs at the front.

THE POWER PACK

C-Series improved

Healey modified the Austin C-Series engine built for sedans like the Austin A90. It has a cast-iron block and cylinder head with a single block-mounted camshaft and conventional rocker-driven overhead valves. The camshaft profile is modified and the cylinder head is improved to increase power, which ranges from the 124 bhp of the Austin-Healey 100/6 to the 148 bhp of the final 3000 variant, which could also boast 165 lb-ft of torque. With triple Weber carburetors for competition, 210 bhp is possible.

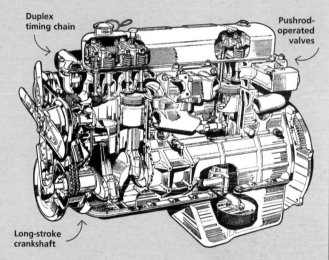

Duplex timing chain
Pushrod-operated valves
Long-stroke crankshaft

Ultimate mark

The last, the best, and definitely the fastest of the 3000 line is the MkIII. It has an improved interior, wooden dashboard, power up from 131 bhp to 148 bhp, plus a revised chassis which improves the rear suspension and better locates the back axle.

Best interior and most power make the MkIII the one to have.

Austin-Healey 3000 🇬🇧

This hybrid designed by Donald Healey and incorporating Austin running gear helped make the 3000 one of the greatest British sports cars ever assembled.

Knock-on wire wheels

Traditional knock-on center-lock wire wheels are the usual fitment on the Austin-Healey, although bolt-on steel disc wheels were available.

Austin engine

All the 'Big Healeys', as they were commonly known, use modified cast-iron Austin engines. They are uncomplicated overhead-valve designs, but are tuneable and very strong.

Front disc brakes

Early Austin-Healeys were drum braked but from 1959 more effective servo-assisted discs were fitted at the front.

In-house styling

Donald Healey relied on his own company to style the original Healey 100, and much of that style lived on in the 3000.

Poor ground clearance

Austin-Healeys are notorious for their poor ground clearance and the exhaust system is particularly vulnerable. This was a great problem for the rally cars and one reason why clearance was improved in 1964.

Two-seaters and 2+2s

From 1962 the two-seater option was deleted and all the 3000 MkII and MkIII models were 2+2s, so occasional passengers could be squeezed in.

Live rear axle

Donald Healey did not want the expense and complication of independent rear suspension and used a live axle. At one time there was a Panhard rod but that was discarded after 1964 and radius arms were fitted.

Cam-and-peg steering

Although the smaller Austin-Healey Sprite uses rack-and-pinion steering, the 3000 has a less precise cam-and-peg system because it was easier to accommodate with the big six-cylinder engine.

Underslung chassis

The chassis was designed for a low, sleek look with the rear axle mounted above the chassis rails.

Specifications
1964 Austin-Healey 3000 MkIII

ENGINE

Type: In-line six cylinder
Construction: Cast-iron block and head
Valve gear: Two in-line valves per cylinder operated by single block-mounted camshaft, pushrods and rockers
Bore and stroke: 3.26 in. x 3.50 in.
Displacement: 2,912 cc
Compression ratio: 9.0:1
Induction system: Two SU carburetors
Maximum power: 148 bhp at 5,250 rpm
Maximum torque: 165 lb-ft at 3,500 rpm

TRANSMISSION

Four-speed manual with overdrive on third and fourth gear

BODY/CHASSIS

X-braced ladder-frame chassis with steel 2+2 convertible body

SPECIAL FEATURES

The left-exiting exhaust on this car indicates that this is a left-hand-drive model. Around 90 percent of 3000s were exported.
The big six-cylinder engine generates a lot of heat and the competition cars have large vents behind the front wheels to help cooling.

RUNNING GEAR

Steering: Cam-and-peg
Front suspension: Double wishbones, coil springs, lever arm shocks and anti-roll bar
Rear suspension: Live axle with semi-elliptic leaf springs, lever arm shocks and radius arms
Brakes: Discs (front), drums (rear)
Wheels: Knock-on center-lock wire spoke 4.5 in. x 15 in.
Tires: Crossply 5.9 in. x 15 in.

DIMENSIONS

Length: 157.5 in. **Width:** 60.5 in.
Wheelbase: 92 in. **Height:** 50 in.
Track: 48.8 in. (front), 50 in. (rear)
Weight: 2,549 lbs.

BMW M1

Built in small numbers and too late for the racing formula it was designed for, the M1 was turned into BMW's first mid-engined, street-legal supercar with a 277-bhp, twin-cam six.

"...designed as a race car."

"At high speeds, you can feel that the M1 was designed as a racing car. It's as solid as a rock with great reserves of power everywhere. Unfortunately, it is simply too heavy to be a competitive racing car. It takes a lot of effort to drive the M1, with both the clutch and brake needing a firm push...though that's a small penalty. Its steering feel and response is pure BMW, rewarding you with endless confidence and unflappable poise."

The M1's disappointingly unattractive cabin hasn't stood the test of time in the way that the ageless Giugiaro exterior shape has.

Milestones

1972 Paul Bracq, head of BMW styling, creates the Turbo Coupe concept car. The head of BMW Motorsport feels the design could be modified to create a racing car to contest Group 4 endurance events. Giugiaro is asked to style the car.

Giorgetto Giugiaro styled the M1 for BMW.

1978 After many delays, the M1 appears at the Paris Show.

The M635CSi and M1 share same basic 24-valve, six-cylinder engine, but the coupe has more power.

1979 Too late and too heavy to be a competitive racer, BMW and FOCA arrange for the M1 to star in the one-marque 'Procar' series to support Grands Prix.

1981 Production ends after 450 cars have been produced—397 road cars and 53 racers.

UNDER THE SKIN

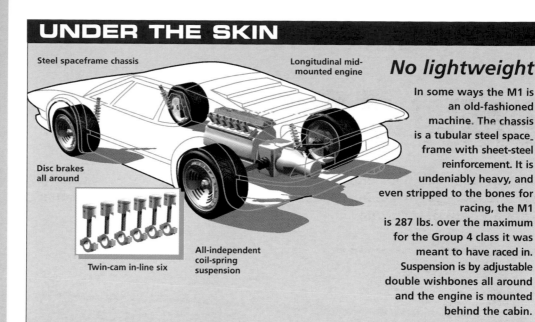

Steel spaceframe chassis

Longitudinal mid-mounted engine

Disc brakes all around

Twin-cam in-line six

All-independent coil-spring suspension

No lightweight

In some ways the M1 is an old-fashioned machine. The chassis is a tubular steel space frame with sheet-steel reinforcement. It is undeniably heavy, and even stripped to the bones for racing, the M1 is 287 lbs. over the maximum for the Group 4 class it was meant to have raced in. Suspension is by adjustable double wishbones all around and the engine is mounted behind the cabin.

Born in the 1960s

The M1's straight-six is a direct descendent of BMW's six from the late-1960s. It grew progressively larger and more powerful. For the M1, it has a new four-valve twin-cam head, twin chain-driven overhead camshafts and 3.5-liter displacement. It was unusual for a racing engine to have a cast-iron block and it is an immensely strong unit—the proposed Group 5 turbo version could produce 700 bhp compared with the road car's 277 bhp. The 24-valve engine was later used in the M635CSi (286 bhp) and the M5 (315 bhp).

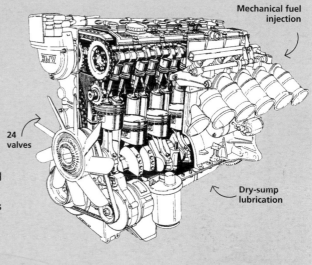

Mechanical fuel injection

24 valves

Dry-sump lubrication

Effective racer

Racing M1s were tuned to almost 200-bhp more than the road car, and their engines could rev to 9,000 rpm. Although it was an overweight racer, it could still be effective. Hans-Joachim Stuck's M1 led more potent cars at Le Mans one year.

The M1 provided plenty of excitement, running in Procar and Group 4 circuits.

BMW M1

It might not look as spectacular as its exotic Ferrari and Lamborghini rivals, but don't let that fool you. The M1 has one major advantage—it was designed as a real racing car.

Tubular steel chassis

Originally, it made sense to farm out the chassis construction to Lamborghini because they had far more experience than BMW in building tubular steel chassis. Eventually Marchesi of Modena made the chassis.

Fiberglass bodywork

All the M1 body panels are fiberglass and they are both riveted and bonded to the tubular steel frame. The body was produced by Italian company TIR (Transformazione Italiana Resina) to a very high standard.

Twin-cam straight-six

In street-legal form the BMW's six-cylinder, twin-cam engine produces 277 bhp from 3.5 liters.

Pirelli P7 tires

The low-profile Pirelli P7 tire was a huge advance in its day and the car's suspension was set up to suit the tire's characteristics.

Slatted engine cover

Hot air from the engine compartment escapes between these large slats. Rearward vision is very good for a mid-engined supercar, and a glass window behind the driver's head insulates the cockpit from the engine bay.

Air intakes

Slots just behind the nearside, rear window feed air to the engine's induction system. The matching slots on the other side are for engine bay ventilation.

Classic grill

The distinctive BMW grill was kept for the M1 and it is functional because both the radiator and the engine oil cooler are at the front. After the air passes over them, it exits through the vents on top of the hood.

Servo brakes

Street-legal M1s have servo-assisted brakes but these were left off the racers, although the driver could adjust the brake balance between front and rear wheels.

Double-wishbone suspension

Most BMWs have some form of semi-trailing arm suspension at the rear but the M1 is different, with racing-type double wishbones in the front and rear.

Specifications
1980 BMW M1

ENGINE
Type: Straight-six twin cam
Construction: Cast iron block and alloy head
Valve gear: Four valves per cylinder operated by two chain-driven overhead camshafts
Bore and stroke: 3.68 in. x 3.31 in.
Displacement: 3,453 cc
Compression ratio: 9.0:1
Induction system: Bosch-Kugelfischer mechanical fuel injection
Maximum power: 277 bhp at 6,500 rpm
Maximum torque: 239 lb-ft at 5,000 rpm

TRANSMISSION
ZF five-speed manual

BODY/CHASSIS
Fiberglass two-door, two-seat coupe body with tubular steel chassis

SPECIAL FEATURES

Rear screen louvers afforded reasonable rearward vision and helped to keep engine temperatures down.

Dated wheel with Pirelli P7s that are narrow by today's standards.

RUNNING GEAR
Steering: Rack-and-pinion
Front suspension: Double wishbones, coil springs, telescopic shocks and anti-roll bar
Rear suspension: Double wishbones, coil springs, telescopic shocks and anti-roll bar
Brakes: Vented discs front and rear
    Wheels: Alloy, 7 in. x 16 in. (front), 8 in. x 16 in. (rear)
    Tires: Pirelli P7, 205/55 VR16 (front), 225/50 VR16 (rear)

DIMENSIONS
    Length: 171.7 in. **Width:** 71.7 in.
    Height: 44.9 in. **Wheelbase:** 100.8 in.
    Track: 61 in. (front), 60.9 in. (rear)
Weight: 3,122 lbs.

BMW Z3

The world is once again full of small sports cars, but in the Z3, BMW has one of the very best. It's compact and a joy to handle. James Bond was happy with his and you would be, too.

"...incredibly nimble."

"There can't be many sports cars easier to drive fast than the tiny Z3. It's perfectly balanced and incredibly nimble; the steering is precise, with loads of feel. The Z3 is nearly foolproof to drive, and even with it switched out, the chassis can handle all 138 bhp with no effort. The levels of grip are so high that only the fearsome 321-bhp M Roadster has the power to unstick the rear end: The 138-bhp 1.9-liter car has a surplus of grip over power. Even when travelling beyond 100 mph, the Z3 feels rock steady and as solid as a sedan."

The dashboard shares switches and gauges with its sedan car brothers. The interior of Z3 1.9 is less exciting than the stylish exterior.

Milestones

1936 The 328 appears, making BMW's name as a sports-car manufacturer of the highest quality. In five years, BMW builds 462 328s.

1955 BMW's purest postwar sports car is the 507. Unfortunately, the beautiful open V8 roadster is too expensive to sell more than 252 cars.

Some styling cues from the 1950s 507 carried over to the new Z3.

1986 Like the 507, the BMW Z1 proves too expensive, although 8,000 are built up to 1991.

Z1 started out as a test bed for BMW's new Z-axle.

1992 BMW plans to build a factory, in Spartanburg, South Carolina.

1996 Z3 production starts. Later in the year, the powerful six-cylinder 2.8 Roadster is unveiled.

1997 BMW launches its fearsome 321-bhp M Roadster.

UNDER THE SKIN

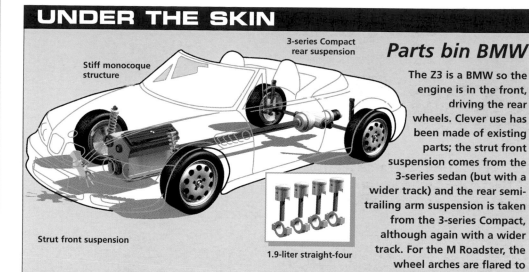

3-series Compact rear suspension

Stiff monocoque structure

Strut front suspension

1.9-liter straight-four

Parts bin BMW

The Z3 is a BMW so the engine is in the front, driving the rear wheels. Clever use has been made of existing parts; the strut front suspension comes from the 3-series sedan (but with a wider track) and the rear semi-trailing arm suspension is taken from the 3-series Compact, although again with a wider track. For the M Roadster, the wheel arches are flared to cover the wider tires.

THE POWER PACK

Efficient four

The new 1.9-liter four-cylinder is BMW's largest four cylinder. It's a 16-valve unit with twin chain-driven cams and hydraulic lifters. It's designed to maximize torque thanks to its variable-length intake manifold, which is effectively long at low rpm to improve torque (an excellent 133 lb-ft), and short at high rpm to help outright power. The engine is also designed to minimize friction; this helps both power output and fuel consumption, which is an impressive 29.4 mpg.

Four valves per cylinder

Variable-length intake manifolds

Twin chain-driven camshafts

M-Power

Good though the 1.9 model is, the Z3's handling and road holding are so good you really need the bigger 2.8-liter straight-six model, or ideally, the M (Motorsport) Roadster to really appreciate the car's fine chassis. The 321-bhp Roadster covers 0-60 mph in only 5.2 seconds, on its way to its governed top speed of 155 mph.

The M Roadster delivers outstanding performance.

BMW Z3

The Z3 is everything you expect from BMW, but in a smaller package. It's only the size of a Mazda Miata, but it's got the handling and road holding capability to handle a 321-bhp straight-six engine with ease.

Semi-trailing arm suspension

Although BMW now produces more advanced rear suspension systems, the Z3 uses the company's traditional semi-trailing arm design because it's more space efficient and does not effect its handling.

Equal weight distribution

Although the engine and transmission are in the front, they are mounted well back, so the weight distribution is still 50/50. This helps to make the Z3's steering very responsive, and lessens the front-engined car's natural inclination to understeer.

Twin-cam engine

The 1.9 model is powered by a 138-bhp twin-cam engine with 16 valves, designed for high torque, good gas mileage as well as power.

Crush-proof windshield pillars

The Z3's windshield pillars are very thick, which helps make them stronger. They are also reinforced with steel tubes inside to form a very strong roll-over hoop if the car overturns.

Galvanized chassis

The Z3's bodyshell is galvanized for long-term rust protection, and the floorpan is made of high-strength steel to help make the open car as stiff as possible.

Long wheelbase

Although the Z3 is small, the wheelbase is quite long to minimize the overhangs at each end. This helps give the BMW its excellent handling and road holding abilities.

Alloy wheels

Base Z3 comes with steel wheels, but the middle of the range 1.9-liter model comes with 7-inch x 15-inch, light-alloy wheels.

Bolt-on panels

To make the car cheaper and easier to repair, the Z3's external body panels are bolted, rather than welded, in place.

Tuned bumper

Convertibles are more prone to shaking and vibration than open cars. Weights in the rear bumper oscillate to cancel out unwanted vibrations running through the car's structure.

ENGINE

Type: In-line four cylinder
Construction: Cast-iron block and alloy cylinder head
Valve gear: Four valves per cylinder operated by twin overhead camshafts and hydraulic lifters
Bore and stroke: 3.35 in. x 3.29 in.
Displacement: 1,895 cc
Compression ratio: 10.0:1
Induction system: Digital Motor Electronics M5.2 electronic fuel injection
Maximum power: 138 bhp at 6,000 rpm
Maximum torque 133 lb-ft at 4,300 rpm

TRANSMISSION

Five-speed manual

BODY/CHASSIS

Galvanized steel monocoque with bolt-on steel panels. Two-door, two-seat convertible body

SPECIAL FEATURES

To show that the Z3 comes from an old, established line of sports cars, BMW incorporated the same design of side vents as found on its 1955 507.

The top of the Z3 series, the M Roadster uses the 3.2-liter, 321-bhp, six-cylinder engine from the M3—giving it incredible acceleration.

RUNNING GEAR

Steering: Rack-and-pinion
Front suspension: MacPherson struts and anti-roll bar
Rear suspension: Semi-trailing arms, coil springs, telescopic shocks and anti-roll bar
Brakes: Discs, 11.3 in. dia. (front) and 10.7 in. dia. (rear) with ABS standard
Wheels: Alloy 7 in. x 15 in.
Tires: 205/60 R15

DIMENSIONS

Length: 158.5 in.   **Width:** 66.6 in.
Height: 50.7 in.   **Wheelbase:** 96.3 in.
Track: 55.6 in. (front), 56.3 in. (rear)
Weight: 2,723 lbs.

Bugatti EB110

Ettore Bugatti's pre-war supercars inspired one man, Romano Artioli, to reform the company and build a car that Ettore himself might have built if he had lived in our age: the incredible quad-turbo V12 EB110.

"...cutting-edge art."

"This is a staggering tour-de-force supercar in the ultimate sense of the word. But as you pull onto the Autostrada, and the four turbochargers summon the silky V12 to sing in your ears, you notice how civilized this all feels. Yes, this is a mid-engined, all-wheel drive, half-million dollar machine. But in your hands, all this cutting-edge technology combines with art as only a true Italian masterpiece can."

Bugatti made the EB110 one of the easiest supercars to drive with its light controls and outstanding high-speed stability.

Milestones

1956 Bugatti ends production with the unsuccessful Type 101; Ettore Bugatti himself had died in 1947.

1987 Romano Artioli acquires the use of the Bugatti name and builds a new factory in Campogalliano near Modena, Italy rather than Molsheim, France where Bugatti was originally based.

1991 the EB110 is launched on September 15 with a spectacular party in Paris. EB stands for Ettore Bugatti and 110 for the 110th anniversary of his birth.

Standard EB110 GT next to the lightweight EB110S.

1992 The EB110 becomes the world's fastest production car, rivaling the Jaguar XJ220 with a speed of 212 mph. The sports version of the EB110 appears, the EB110S.

1994 The EB110S is renamed the EB110SS (Super Sport) and has a power output of 611 bhp and 477 lb-ft of torque, to give a claimed top speed of 221 mph.

1995 Sales of the EB110 never reach the over-optimistic projected levels and the company finally goes into receivership.

UNDER THE SKIN

Carbon fiber structure

The EB110 has a carbon fiber tub for two reasons: the material is extremely strong and also far lighter than steel or alloy. It covers a four-wheel drive system with the gearbox ahead of the mid-mounted engine and connected to the front differentials via a torque tube. Only 27 percent of the drive goes to the front wheels.

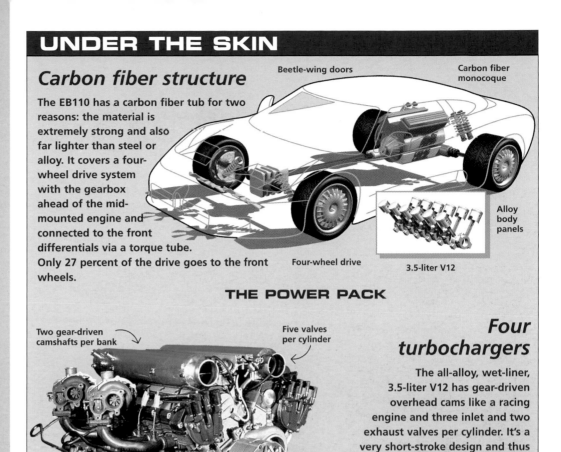

Beetle-wing doors

Carbon fiber monocoque

Alloy body panels

Four-wheel drive

3.5-liter V12

THE POWER PACK

Two gear-driven camshafts per bank

Five valves per cylinder

Four IHI turbochargers

All-alloy construction

Dry sump lubrication

Four turbochargers

The all-alloy, wet-liner, 3.5-liter V12 has gear-driven overhead cams like a racing engine and three inlet and two exhaust valves per cylinder. It's a very short-stroke design and thus revs very high, maximum power being produced only 200 rpm short of its maximum engine speed of 8,200 rpm. Instead of the more common twin turbo it uses four small Japanese IHI units. The engine uses silicon-impregnated cylinder liners to reduce friction between piston and cylinder wall.

Supersport

The S stood for Supersport. It was designed for international GT racing and had a fixed rear wing, no rear side windows and stiffened suspension. The 110SS, as it was later known, was 441 lbs. lighter thanks to carbon fiber body panels, Plexiglas side windows and a stripped interior. An extra 40 bhp raised the already impressive top speed to 221 mph.

The earth-shattering EB110S: 441 lbs. lighter than the standard car.

Bugatti EB110

Despite the name, Bugatti was originally a French company. However, when it reformed in the 1990s, it was Italian-owned and the EB110 rivaled other Italian greats, the Ferrari F40 and Lamborghini Diablo.

Four-wheel drive

The Bugatti's 552 bhp is fed to all four wheels, although not in equal amounts: 63 percent of the drive goes to the rear and 37 percent to the front.

Six-speed transmission

To enable the driver to exploit all the power from the rev-happy V12, the EB110 has a six-speed close-ratio transmission mounted in front of the engine.

Four turbochargers

To avoid turbo lag at low engine speeds, the EB110 has no fewer than four small intercooled IHI turbos, two for each bank of cylinders.

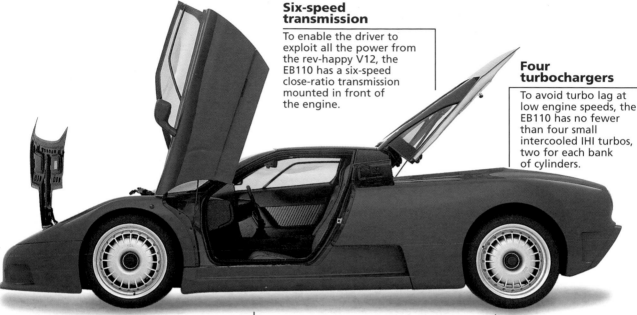

Carbon fiber chassis

Even before the advanced McLaren F1 appeared, the EB110 had a main structural 'tub' or chassis made of carbon fiber, making it incredibly strong.

Special Michelin tires

Bugatti's close relationship with Michelin resulted in special ultra low-profile MXX3 tires for the EB110, fitted to alloy wheels inspired by those fitted to the pre-war Bugatti Royale.

Quad-cam V12

The EB110's 3.5-liter V12 revs to 8,200 rpm and produces as much power as the early Cosworth DFV Formula One engines.

Traditional Bugatti grill

Bugatti's horseshoe shaped radiator opening was retained for the EB110, to give it unmistakable links to Bugatti's past.

Anti-pollution devices

Four turbos are complemented by four catalytic convertors and an oil vapor collector to make the EB110 as eco-friendly as possible.

Twin rear shocks

To give the best wheel control, the EB110 uses two shocks on each side of the car's rear double wishbone suspension.

Alloy bodywork

To save weight, the body is made from lightweight aluminum alloy, usually painted traditional Bugatti blue, although some EB110s are silver.

Specifications
1993 Bugatti EB110

ENGINE
Type: V12, quad-cam
Construction: Light alloy block and heads with wet cylinder liners
Valve gear: Five valves per cylinder (three inlet, two exhaust) operated by four overhead camshafts
Bore and stroke: 3.3 in. x 2.2 in.
Displacement: 3,500 cc
Compression ratio: 7.5:1
Induction system: Bugatti multi-port fuel injection with four IHI turbos
Maximum power: 552 bhp at 8,000 rpm
Maximum torque: 450 lb-ft at 3,750 rpm

TRANSMISSION
Six-speed manual

BODY/CHASSIS
Alloy two-door, two-seat coupe with carbon fiber monocoque chassis

SPECIAL FEATURES

Like the Lamborghini Diablo, the EB110 has 'butterfly' doors. On a car this wide, it would be almost impossible to open conventional doors in a standard size parking space or garage.

RUNNING GEAR
Steering: Rack-and-pinion
Front suspension: Twin wishbones, coil springs, telescopic shocks and anti-roll bar
Rear suspension: Twin wishbones, with twin coil spring/shock units per side
Brakes: Vented discs (front and rear), 12.7 in. with ABS
Wheels: Magnesium alloy 9 in. x 18 in. (front),12 in. x 18 in. (rear)
Tires: Michelin 245/40 (front) and 325/30 (rear)

DIMENSIONS
Length: 173.2 in.
Width: 76.4 in.
Wheelbase: 100.4 in.
Height: 44.3 in.
Track: 61 in. (front), 63.7 in. (rear)
Weight: 3,571 lbs.

Chevrolet **CAMARO Z28**

The legendary Z28 moniker has stuck with the Camaro well into its fourth generation. Since that magic three-figure code first appeared in 1967, it has always meant the same thing to buyers—added performance.

"...strong performance bias."

"Once you've settled yourself into the plush leather interior of the Z28, you realize that you're in a car with a strong performance bias. Start the car up and the V8 engine signals its intentions through its robust exhaust note. The deep-chested 305 cubic inch engine hauls you rapidly towards the horizon. Its suspension is tight through turns thanks to imprvments over the base Camaro model. With the 1LE package, handling is upgraded even further."

Red was one of three interior colors for the 1992 Heritage edition featured on the following pages.

Milestones

1982 Chevrolet launches the third-generation Camaro to replace the previous 12-year-old model. It is available with a four-, six- or an eight-cylinder engine.

Second-generation Z28s continued until 1981, and still offer decent performance. The fastest is the 1970 LT-1™ Z28.

1985 IROC-Z is added to the Camaro line. The new model features a special fascia, body skirts, and distinctive 16-inch cast-alloy wheels.

1987 The convertible returns to the range and is available in all Camaro trim levels.

The fourth generation Z28 appeared in 1993 and was the best balanced Camaro yet.

1988 The Z28 is dropped, only to be revived for 1991.

1992 Production of the third-generation Camaro ends to make way for the sleek, new fourth-generation model.

UNDER THE SKIN

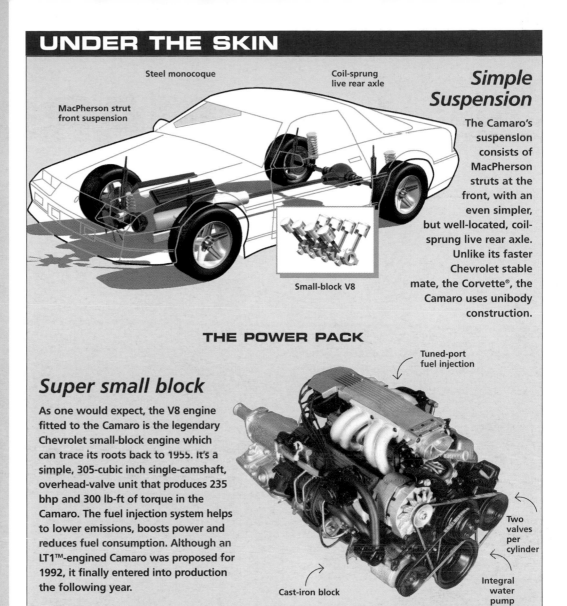

Steel monocoque

Coil-sprung live rear axle

MacPherson strut front suspension

Small-block V8

Simple Suspension

The Camaro's suspension consists of MacPherson struts at the front, with an even simpler, but well-located, coil-sprung live rear axle. Unlike its faster Chevrolet stable mate, the Corvette®, the Camaro uses unibody construction.

THE POWER PACK

Super small block

As one would expect, the V8 engine fitted to the Camaro is the legendary Chevrolet small-block engine which can trace its roots back to 1955. It's a simple, 305-cubic inch single-camshaft, overhead-valve unit that produces 235 bhp and 300 lb-ft of torque in the Camaro. The fuel injection system helps to lower emissions, boosts power and reduces fuel consumption. Although an LT1™-engined Camaro was proposed for 1992, it finally entered into production the following year.

Tuned-port fuel injection

Two valves per cylinder

Integral water pump

Cast-iron block

Final fling

The last year for the third-generation Camaro was 1992. The two main models available were the RS® that had a 189-cubic inch V6 as standard or with an optional V8, and the high-performance Z28. Both coupe and convertible body styles were available.

By 1992 the Camaro was a two-model range: the RS™ (shown) and the Z28.

41

Chevrolet CAMARO Z28 🇺🇸

Always a top seller, the Camaro has all the right ingredients to satisfy the enthusiastic driver—power, performance, fine rear-drive handling and head-turning looks.

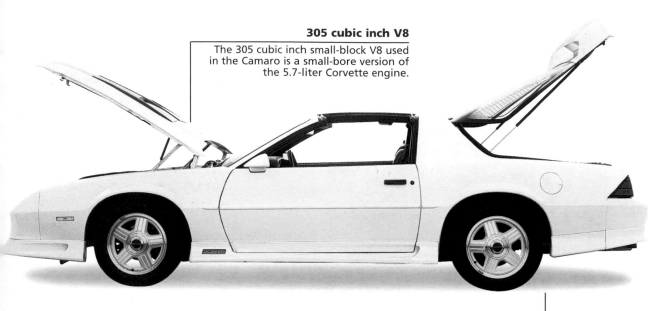

305 cubic inch V8

The 305 cubic inch small-block V8 used in the Camaro is a small-bore version of the 5.7-liter Corvette engine.

Large hatchback

The luggage area of the Camaro is easily accessed through the lift-up hatch. More luggage space is available when the rear seat is folded forward.

Live rear axle

The live rear axle is coil sprung and well located by longitudinal links to help prevent wheel hop during hard acceleration. A Panhard rod is used for lateral location.

Body kit

To keep the third-generation Camaro looking as fresh as possible during its 10-year run, Chevrolet designers used a bolt-on body kit of extra spoilers and side skirts.

Limited-slip differential

To help prevent wheelspin, a limited-slip differential is standard on the 1992 Camaro Z28 and has a 3.42:1 rear axle ratio.

Heritage appearance package

To celebrate the Camaro's 25th birthday, in 1992 all models were finished with the Heritage appearance package, available in red, white or black.

Specifications

1992 Chevrolet Camaro Z28

ENGINE

Type: V8

Construction: Cast-iron block and heads

Valve gear: Single camshaft operating two valves per cylinder

Bore and stroke: 3.74 in. x 3.48 in.

Displacement: 305 c.i.

Compression ratio: 9.5:1

Induction system: Electronic fuel injection

Maximum power: 235 bhp at 4,400 rpm

Maximum torque: 300 lb-ft at 3,200 rpm

TRANSMISSION

Five-speed manual

BODY/CHASSIS

Two-door coupe monocoque

SPECIAL FEATURES

Hood stripes are part of the Heritage appearance package to celebrate the Camaro's 25th birthday.

The rear spoiler is as much for looks as for its aerodynamic effect.

RUNNING GEAR

Steering: Recirculating ball

Front suspension: Independent with MacPherson struts, separate coil springs, telescopic shocks and anti-roll bar

Rear suspension: Live axle on longitudinal links with Panhard rod, coil springs and telescopic shocks

Brakes: Discs (front), drums or optional discs (rear)

Wheels: Alloy, 14-in. dia.

Tires: 205/70 R14

DIMENSIONS

Length: 192.6 in.   **Width:** 72.4 in.

Height: 51.5 in.   **Wheelbase:** 101 in.

Track: 60 in. (front), 60.9 in. (rear)

Weight: 3,105 lbs.

Chevrolet **CORVETTE**

Some might say that the Corvette looks good enough and goes fast enough as standard. Others, though, will always crave individuality or more speed from their car and set out to create their version of the ideal Vette™.

"...always entertaining."

"A Corvette will always be entertaining to drive, whatever the year, whatever the power output. On these late cars, it's just a case of rechipping the engine management system to boost the power and give you the extra performance you need. Heads turn as you plant your foot and the deep-chested V8 rumble changes to a hard-edged howl from the aftermarket exhaust system and the car tears away. The standard Corvette steering is retained and handling is just as good, but the ride suffers on the lowered suspension, especially on poorly surfaced roads."

Corvette interior looks good as stock, especially with the optional leather bucket seats.

Milestones

1953 First Corvette introduced with a straight-six engine and fiberglass body.

1955 In response to the launch of the V8 Ford Thunderbird, Chevrolet added the new 265-cubic inch small-block V8 engine.

The third generation Corvettes lasted from 1968 through 1982.

1963 New restyled Sting Ray® is launched. The chassis is new and the car features all-around independent suspension. A larger big-block V8 engine is added in 1965.

1968 Corvette restyled again and is known as the Stingray from 1969.

There are many specialists who modify Corvettes. This car has been modified by Kaminari Design.

1984 Corvette receives a total redesign with new styling, chassis and new front and rear suspension. From 1985 to 1992, the standard engine is the L98 350 V8.

1990 Ultimate factory Corvette development arrives, the 379-bhp ZR-1.

UNDER THE SKIN

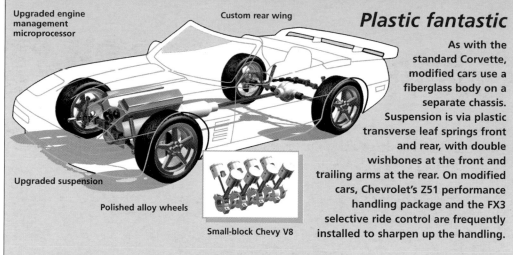

Upgraded engine management microprocessor

Custom rear wing

Upgraded suspension

Polished alloy wheels

Small-block Chevy V8

Plastic fantastic

As with the standard Corvette, modified cars use a fiberglass body on a separate chassis. Suspension is via plastic transverse leaf springs front and rear, with double wishbones at the front and trailing arms at the rear. On modified cars, Chevrolet's Z51 performance handling package and the FX3 selective ride control are frequently installed to sharpen up the handling.

THE POWER PACK

Ultimate power

The ultimate engine for a modified Corvette is the LT5 unit installed in the mighty ZR-1. With two cams per cylinder bank operating four valves per cylinder, the LT5 produces an incredible 379 bhp, while still offering similar levels of driveability as a standard, small-block engined Corvette. The capacity remains the same at 350 cubic inches. Other modified Corvettes use the single camshaft small-block V8 (shown here) with an array of tuning equipment. Later cars can have their power boosted by simply upgrading the microchip in the engine control management system.

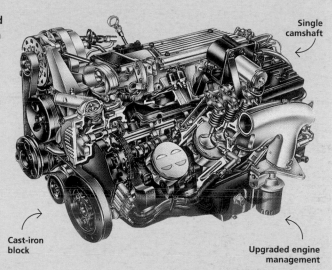

Single camshaft

Cast-iron block

Upgraded engine management

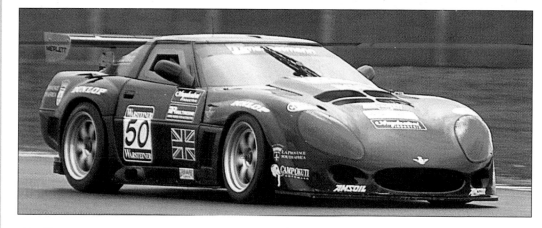

Callaway

The ultimate in modified Corvettes is the Callaway Corvette. Early models used turbochargers to give a boost in power, but later versions relied on increased capacity. In 1994, Callaway launched the Corvette-based C7R racer with carbon fiber bodywork.

This C7R is the ultimate Corvette-based car with nearly 660 bhp.

Chevrolet CORVETTE

The Corvette holds a place next to any American's heart. Some like their car standard, others feel the need for a little personalization. Modifications range from the subtle to the outrageous.

'Chipped' engine

The Corvette has a sophisticated computerized engine management system, making it difficult for the amateur mechanic to tune the engine. The easiest way to raise power is to replace the control module with an upgraded unit which controls ignition timing and the fuel metering.

Leather bucket seats

Although some modified Vettes feature custom upholstery, many opt for the leather bucket seats, which hold the driver firmly in place under the high cornering forces the Corvette is capable of generating. The driver's seat is electrically adjustable.

ABS brakes

Despite the boost from the tweaked engine, the Corvette's standard brakes are sufficient. For extra stopping power, the larger 13-inch front discs from the ZR-1 can be used.

Transmission

This car has the standard four-speed plus overdrive gearbox, but the ultimate Corvette transmission package would use the optional six-speed manual gearbox and low ratio performance axle.

Suspension

Adding Chevrolet's own Performance Handling Package improves the car's handling further. There is also a Selective Ride Control system available which allows the driver to select one of three different shock settings.

Body modifications

Because it's fiberglass, the Corvette's bodyshell is relatively easy to modify. This subtle rear deck wing has been added by the owner.

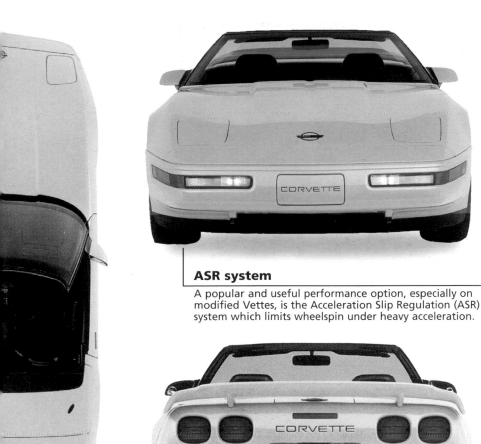

ASR system

A popular and useful performance option, especially on modified Vettes, is the Acceleration Slip Regulation (ASR) system which limits wheelspin under heavy acceleration.

Upgraded exhaust system

Extra horsepower and a whole lot of V8 rumble can be released by adding an aftermarket system. This car uses a B&B Tri-Flow stainless-steel exhaust system.

Polished alloy wheels

Although this is a 1994 car, the owner has installed the wheels from a 1996 Corvette. The 17-inch rims have been polished to a mirror finish.

1994 Modified Chevrolet Corvette

ENGINE

Type: V8, LT1
Construction: Cast-iron block and aluminum cylinder heads
Valve gear: Two valves per cylinder actuated by a single block-mounted camshaft via pushrods, rocker arms and hydraulic lifters
Bore and stroke: 4 in. x 3.48 in.
Displacement: 350 c.i.
Compression ratio: 10.1:1
Induction system: Computer-controlled sequential fuel injection
Maximum power: 330 bhp at 5,500 rpm
Maximum torque: 340 lb-ft at 4,000 rpm

TRANSMISSION

Four-speed plus overdrive automatic transmission

BODY/CHASSIS

Two-seater fiberglass convertible body on 'uniframe' chassis

SPECIAL FEATURES

The owner of this Corvette has subtly modified the body with a color-coded wing added to the rear deck.

An upgraded engine control module gives a significant increase in power.

RUNNING GEAR

Steering: Power-assisted rack and pinion
Front suspension: Double wishbones with semi-elliptic fiberglass transverse spring, telescopic shock absorbers
Rear suspension: Five link with trailing arms and semi-elliptic fiberglass transverse leaf spring, telescopic shock absorbers
Brakes: Discs, front and rear with anti-lock system
Wheels: 1996 model chromed alloy, 17 in. x 8.5 in. (front) 17 in. x 9.5 in. (rear)
Tires: Goodyear Eagle GS-C, 255/45ZR-17 (front), 285/40ZR-17 (rear)

DIMENSIONS

Length: 178.5 in.   **Width:** 70.7 in.
Height: 46.3 in.   **Wheelbase:** 96.2 in.
Track: 56.8 in. (front), 59.1 in. (rear)
Weight: 3,504 lbs.

JAPAN 1969–1974

Datsun 240Z

In one fell swoop Datsun slayed the American sports car market with the 240Z. It had everything: beautiful looks, a punchy six-cylinder engine, great handling, superb build quality and a bargain price.

"...the essence of sportiness."

"Compared to rival machinery from the early 1970s, the 240Z is quick. The six-cylinder engine pulls strongly through the well-chosen gear ratios and with the long-legged, five-speed transmission cruising is pleasant. Gas mileage is also surprisingly good. Fully-independent suspension results in excellent road manners and minimal understeer, with power oversteer readily available. The brakes are sharp and fade-free and the steering responsive."

Deeply-set gauges and a wood-rimmed wheel were fashionable for 1970s sports cars.

Milestones

1969 The 240Z makes its public debut at the Tokyo Motor Show.

1970 Automatic transmission is offered for the first time.

For 1975, the 240 was replaced by the larger-engined 260Z.

1971 Datsun scores a 1-2 in the East African Safari Rally, and the long-nose 240ZG is homologated. Standard cars receive altered differentials, and for the 1972 model year the engine is fitted with revised carburetors.

Despite a bigger engine, the 280ZX produces only 135 bhp.

1973 A 240Z again wins the East African Safari Rally. Road cars receive smog equipment and Federal bumpers.

1974 The 240Z is replaced by the new 260Z.

UNDER THE SKIN

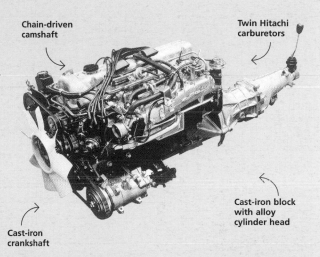

Steel body

MacPherson strut suspension

Standard front disc brakes

Cast-iron in-line six

Jaguar-inspired

Count Albrecht Goertz wanted to produce a car like the Jaguar E-type but in a smaller package. The 240Z follows the Jaguar quite closely, being rear-drive, with a front-mounted in-line six, plus all-independent suspension. The set up includes MacPherson struts, with wide-based lower wishbones at the rear and a front anti-roll bar. Girling front disc brakes are standard.

THE POWER PACK

Straight-six power

The L24 in-line six-cylinder engine was derived from the 1.6-liter Bluebird 510 single overhead-cam four-cylinder unit. It is fairly conventional, with a cast-iron block and alloy head. It features a single chain-driven overhead camshaft, plus twin Hitachi SU-type carburetors. It is quite free-revving, producing its peak output of 150 bhp at a high 6,000 rpm. In Japan it was only available in 2.0-liter form, but export market models had a slightly larger capacity of 2.4 liters. In 1974 it was stroked to 2,565 cc.

Chain-driven camshaft

Twin Hitachi carburetors

Cast-iron block with alloy cylinder head

Cast-iron crankshaft

Pure original

The original 240Z is undoubtedly the most sought after today. Later 260s and 280s are more luxurious, but are also heavier and less exciting to drive. Extremely desirable, but rare, are the lightweight Z432 (Japan only) and 240ZG specials.

Early Zs are characterized by their pure styling and better performance.

Datsun 240Z

Unashamedly created for and targeted at the U.S. market, the 240Z marked the beginning of the modern era of Japanese sports cars. It did almost everything right, and sales went straight through the roof.

High standard of finish

In addition to an attractive price, the Datsun Z's high level of build quality was very impressive. By comparison, European sports cars were not very well put together and could be unreliable in service. The Datsun was a more sensible proposition for everyday use.

Six-cylinder engine

Datsun's punchy in-line six gave impressive performance for a sports car, especially one which sold at such a low price. Unlike some of its rivals, the 240Z's engine was also incredibly strong and reliable.

Hatchback rear

In most sports cars practicality is overlooked, but the 240Z features an opening decklid, complete with spoiler, plus a useful storage area behind the seats. However, space is impeded by the intrusion of the suspension struts and the spare tire.

All-independent suspension

While rivals still used live rear axles and leaf springs, the 240Z was updated with an all-independent suspension front and rear giving the Z outstanding cornering ability.

Handsome styling

The smooth styling of the Z was probably its biggest selling point. Count Albrecht Goertz, who conceived the Z, had a solid track record in recognizing what the American public wanted. Goertz's other achievements include the BMW 507 and the Toyota 2000GT.

Specifications

1971 Datsun 240Z

ENGINE

Type: In-line six-cylinder

Construction: Cast-iron block and alloy head

Valve gear: Two valves per cylinder operated by a chain-driven single overhead camshaft

Bore and stroke: 3.27 in. x 2.9 in.

Displacement: 2,393 cc

Compression ratio: 9.0:1

Induction system: Two Hitachi HJG 46W carburetors

Maximum power: 150 bhp at 6,000 rpm

Maximum torque: 148 lb-ft at 4,400 rpm

TRANSMISSION

Four- or five-speed manual or three-speed automatic

BODY/CHASSIS

Steel monocoque with two-door coupe body

SPECIAL FEATURES

The straight-six engine is reliable, and easily capable of lasting 150,000 miles.

Very few Datsun Zs retain their original wheels and trims. Most are now fitted with aftermarket alloy wheels.

RUNNING GEAR

Steering: Rack-and-pinion

Front suspension: MacPherson struts with coil springs, telescopic shock absorbers and anti-roll bar

Rear suspension: Chapman struts with coil springs, telescopic shock absorbers and anti-roll bar

Brakes: Discs (front), drums (rear)

Wheels: Steel, 14-in. dia.

Tires: 175 x 14 in.

DIMENSIONS

Length: 162.8 in.   **Width:** 64.1 in.

Height: 50.6 in.   **Wheelbase:** 90.7 in.

Track: 53.3 in. (front), 53.0 in. (rear)

Weight: 2,355 lbs.

De Tomaso PANTERA

The combination of an exotic Italian-styled body with the strength, power and reliability of a huge American V8 engine seemed to offer the best of both worlds to some manufacturers, De Tomaso in particular. The Pantera is one of the world's longest-lived supercars.

"Acceleration is shattering."

"That massive engine thunders away just behind your head, shaking the whole car and generating enough heat to make the standard air conditioning absolutely vital. Shifts are made with the ZF 5-speed transaxle, steering is light and handling impressive. The grip on those huge tires is enormous and the Pantera rides flat through the sharpest of turns. Its 5.6-second 0-60 acceleration is shattering and 165 mph top speed is virtually unmatched by any competitor. In fact, the exotic Italian-styled car looks fast even when it's standing still."

The Pantera interior has plush leather seats and instruments that are very easy to see.

Milestones

1969 Ford provides funds to produce the first Pantera. De Tomaso retains European sales rights, while Ford retains the rights in the U.S.

1971 Pantera goes on sale.

The Mangusta was De Tomaso's first V8-engined supercar.

1974 Chassis revisions, better brakes and a 330-bhp 351 'Cleveland' Ford V8 engine are in the European-spec GTS models. Due to emissions regulations, U.S. models produce only 266 bhp. Ford pulls out of the project leaving De Tomaso to build the cars independently.

1982 The GT5 is launched. Tacked-on wheel arch extensions are used to fit wider wheels and tires.

The GT5 gained wheel arch extensions and rear spoiler.

1990 Dramatic revamp is undertaken, although the concept stays the same. The engine is now Ford's popular 5.0 liter that makes 305 bhp with natural aspiration. By adding twin turbochargers, the Pantera makes up to 450 bhp.

UNDER THE SKIN

Mighty monocoque

Unusual for an Italian supercar, the Pantera has a steel monocoque structure. The car was planned to be sold in high volume through Ford dealers, so a separate chassis design would have been too labor-intensive and slow. The big Ford V8 is mounted behind the driver, turning the rear wheels through a rugged ZF five-speed transaxle. Double-wishbone suspension is used on all four wheels.

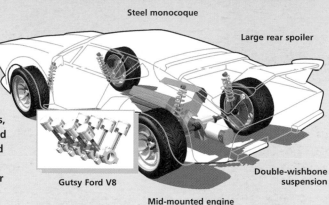

Steel monocoque

Large rear spoiler

Double-wishbone suspension

Mid-mounted engine

Gutsy Ford V8

THE POWER PACK

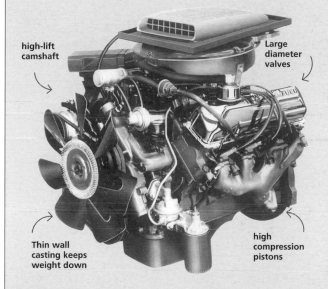

high-lift camshaft

Large diameter valves

Thin wall casting keeps weight down

high compression pistons

Ford power

The best engine to be fitted to the Pantera was the Ford 'Cleveland' V8 (named after the plant where it was built). It is a conventional all-iron V8 with high-lift camshaft and hydraulic lifters, although solid lifters could be specified for higher rpm. Although big, at 5,763 cc, its thin wall casting made it relatively lightweight. The engine could easily be tuned to produce more power with a high compression ratio, big valves, higher lift cams, free-flowing exhaust systems and multiple carburetors rather than one Holley.

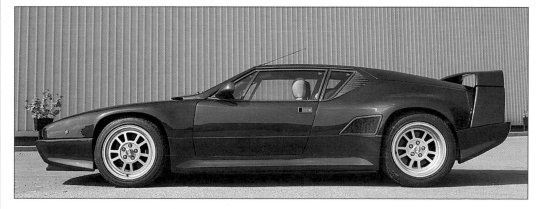

1990s Pantera

The Pantera was totally updated for the 90s with the introduction of the Gandini-styled 450 in 1990. It uses twin turbochargers to boost the power of a smaller 5.0-liter V8 engine to 450 bhp, hence the name. De Tomaso claims a top speed over 180 mph.

Gandini's restyle and twin turbos really brought the Pantera up to date.

De Tomaso **PANTERA**

The Pantera was built tough to survive on the U.S. market, with a simple and strong Ford V8 engine. It proved to be the right approach and the Pantera stayed in production long after it should have become obsolete.

Wishbone suspension

The Pantera featured double-wishbone suspension with telescopic shocks, coil springs and anti-roll bars.

Five-speed transaxle

To better handle the power output of the V8 engine, a strong ZF five-speed transaxle was used, along with a limited slip differential.

Steel monocoque

As it was intended to be built in large numbers for a supercar (Ford hoped for 5,000 a year), it was designed to be built like a mass-production car, with a unitary steel monocoque.

Ford V8 engine

Because the Pantera was to be sold through Ford in the large U.S. market, it used a Ford Cleveland 5,763 cc V8 overhead valve engine design that was used in many early Mustangs.

Front spoiler

Designed to complement that flamboyant extrovert rear wing, the front spoiler plays its part in cutting down the amount of air that can flow under the car.

Carbon fiber rear spoiler

A rear spoiler was optional on the Pantera to provide extra downforce at very high speeds. By the 1980s that spoiler was made of carbon fiber.

Unequal-size wheels

To carry the large rear tires the rear wheels are 13 inches wide, compared with the slimmer 10-inch wide front wheels.

Extra driving lights

Its headlights were never the Pantera's strong suit and the extra driving lights which could be fitted in front of the air dam were a valuable addition.

Specifications
1986 De Tomaso Pantera GT5S

ENGINE

Type: Ford V8
Construction: Cast-iron block and heads
Valve gear: Two valves per cylinder operated by single block-mounted camshaft via pushrods and rockers
Bore and stroke: 4.01 in. x 3.50 in.
Displacement: 5,763 cc
Compression ratio: 10.5:1
Induction system: Single four-barrel Holley 680 cfm carburetor
Maximum power: 350 bhp at 6,000 rpm
Maximum torque: 451 lb-ft at 3,800 rpm

TRANSMISSION

ZF five-speed manual transaxle

BODY/CHASSIS

Steel monocoque two-door, two-seat coupe

SPECIAL FEATURES

Wheel vents in the rear arch extensions redirect cool air to the brakes keeping them from getting too hot and fading at high speeds.

Like the Lamborghini Countach, De Tomaso Panteras came with an optional rear spoiler. It was as much for style as function.

RUNNING GEAR

Steering: Rack-and-pinion
Front suspension: Double wishbones with coil springs, telescopic shocks and anti-roll bar
Rear suspension: Double wishbones, coil springs, telescopic shocks and anti-roll bar
  Brakes: 11.7 in. discs (front) vented 11.2 in. discs (rear)
  Wheels: Alloy, 10 in. x 15 in. (front), 13 in. x 15 in. (rear)
Tires: 285/40 VR15 (front), 345/35 VR15 (rear)

DIMENSIONS

Length: 168.1 in.   **Width:** 77.5 in.
Wheelbase: 99 in.   **Height:** 44.3 in.
Track: 61 in. (front), 62.1 in. (rear)
Weight: 3,202 lbs.

DeLorean DMC

John DeLorean had a dream, to build a sports car that would never rust or corrode. It was finished in brushed stainless steel over a fiberglass body, but the dream quickly turned into a nightmare.

"...adequate, not exciting."

"You sit deep in the somber interior. It's claustrophobic, but it is comfortable enough, as is the ride. Is it quick and sharp enough for a sports car? Not really; there just isn't enough power from the V6 to give either impressive acceleration or top speed. The DMC was intended to provide a futuristic look with its full electronic gadgetry, stainless steel body, and gullwing doors. Unfortunately, its performance isn't as impressive as the car's look suggests."

Lotus-inspired backbone chassis means there's a deep spine through the cockpit. Note the small opening section of the windows.

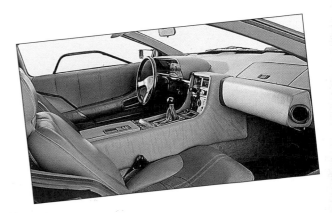

Milestones

1963 Pontiac's chief engineer John DeLorean becomes famous when he creates the GTO which becomes the first true 1960s American 'musclecar.'

Giugiaro's design proposals included a four-door sedan.

1974 After leaving
General Motors, DeLorean founds the John Z. DeLorean Company, the first step on the way to developing his own car.

1976 First prototype,
the Giugiaro-styled DMC12, is assembled.

1978 British Government loans
money to help create a factory in Northern Ireland to manufacture the DeLorean.

1981 Production
begins at the Dumurray factory near Belfast.

1982 Lack of sales
forces the factory into a three-day week. DeLorean goes into receivership in February. By the end of the year there are more than 2,000 cars still unsold.

UNDER THE SKIN

Lotus influence

The Lotus influence is enormous; the backbone chassis is unmistakably a Lotus design very similar to the Esprit's. It looks like a very elongated X, with the V6 engine mounted between the chassis arms at the rear. That is balanced by putting the fuel tank and radiator at the other end of the chassis. There is more Lotus influence in the suspension, which is more compliant than other sports cars, using long semi-trailing arms at the rear.

Rear-mounted engine

Backbone chassis

Semi-trailing arm rear suspension

Renault's alloy V6

THE POWER PACK

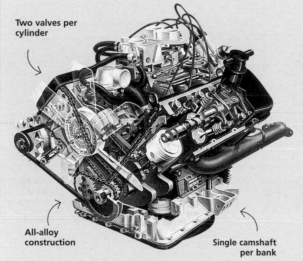

Two valves per cylinder

All-alloy construction

Single camshaft per bank

Bought-in V6

DeLorean used an outside engine, the V6 developed by Peugeot/Renault/Volvo. It is all-alloy with a single overhead camshaft for each bank of cylinders, and only two valves per cylinder, as it wasn't developed as a sporty engine. In U.S. spec it was detuned compared with a European engine which put out 130 bhp from its 2.8 liters, although the torque output was respectable. Renault showed what could be achieved with the engine in the Alpine A310 and the A610, particularly when it was turbocharged.

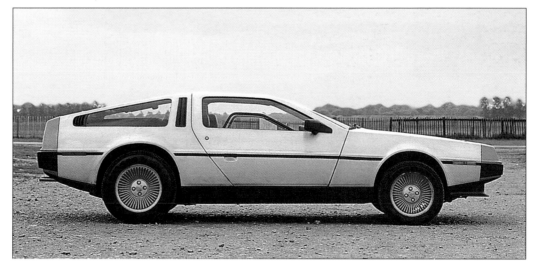

Blown away

DeLorean was well aware he needed more power and so had Legend Industries build a prototype turbocharged DeLorean using two small Japanese IHI turbos. It worked extremely well, giving the car the performance it lacked.

Turbocharging would have given the DeLorean the performance it needed.

DeLorean DMC 🇬🇧

The official name 'Sports Car' was hardly ever used. It showed a lack of imagination, which the design itself did not. With more development and power it could have been a great success.

V6 engine

DeLorean needed to buy his engines 'off the shelf' and the Renault/Peugeot/Volvo V6 was ideal. It was large, yet light enough so it wouldn't spoil the handling.

'Gullwing' doors

John DeLorean was an admirer of the Mercedes-Benz 300SL, and realized the marketing potential of its 'Gullwing' doors.

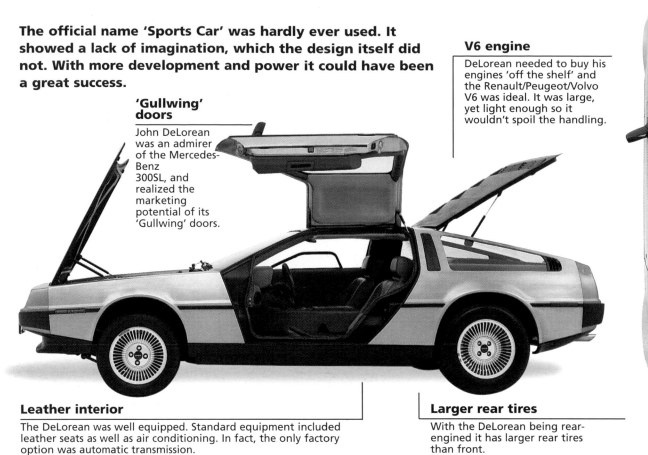

Leather interior

The DeLorean was well equipped. Standard equipment included leather seats as well as air conditioning. In fact, the only factory option was automatic transmission.

Larger rear tires

With the DeLorean being rear-engined it has larger rear tires than front.

Rear weight bias

The rear-mounted engine puts as much as 65 percent of the car's weight over the rear wheels.

Front radiator

With the engine at the back, the logical place for the radiator and the fuel tank is in the front of the car.

Backbone chassis

The backbone chassis is the clearest evidence of Lotus involvement. They had used such a system for years, starting with the original Elan, and its design is very close to the contemporary Esprit's.

Specifications
1981 DeLorean Sports Car

ENGINE

Type: V6

Construction: Alloy block and heads

Valve gear: Two inclined valves per cylinder operated by single chain-driven overhead cam per bank of cylinders

Bore and stroke: 3.58 in. x 2.87 in.

Displacement: 2,849 cc

Compression ratio: 8.8:1

Induction system: Bosch K-Jetronic fuel injection

Maximum power: 145 bhp at 5,500 rpm

Maximum torque: 162 lb-ft at 2,750 rpm

TRANSMISSION

Renault five-speed manual

BODY/CHASSIS

Sheet-steel backbone chassis with fiberglass coupe body covered with stainless steel

SPECIAL FEATURES

To get some fresh air on the road, there are small opening electric windows set in the door.

Relatively low power and low weight means that the rear-mounted engine does not cause poor handling traits.

RUNNING GEAR

Steering: Rack-and-pinion

Front suspension: Double wishbones with coil springs, telescopic shocks, and anti-roll bar

Rear suspension: Semi-trailing arms, coil springs, and telescopic shocks

Brakes: Discs all around, 10.5 in. dia. (front), 10 in. dia. (rear)

Wheels: Alloy 6 in. x 14 in. (front), 8 in. x 15 in. (rear)

Tires: Goodyear NCT 195/60HR14 (front), 235/60HR15 (rear)

DIMENSIONS

Length: 168 in.   **Width:** 78.3 in.

Height: 44.9 in.   **Wheelbase:** 94.89 in.

Track: 62.6 in. (front), 62.5 in. (rear)

Weight: 2,840 lbs.

Dodge VIPER

The Viper was designed as a modern incarnation of the legendary Shelby Cobra of the 1960s—no nonsense, no frills, just big bags of brute power. The massive V10 is the biggest engine currently shoehorned into a production car.

"...a street brawler."

"Some owners describe it as 'a great motor looking for a car.' Cruising at 75 mph, the wind batters you, the exhaust drones, engine and exhaust heat cook your feet. But when you put your foot down, all of the faults disappear. The engine has so much torque it's possible to drive away in 3rd, then shift to 6th at 35 mph. With its eight liters, the V10 actually pulls at 500 rpm. This is a no-holds-barred street brawler that will rattle your fillings and your neighbors' windows."

Functional cockpit with stark white instruments. A very high 6th gear (53 mph per 1,000 rpm) is required to pass California emission laws.

Milestones

1989 The Viper was originally a 'concept car'—a car taken to the motor shows to gauge public reaction. It is shown at the Detroit International Auto Show in January 1989. Public reaction is overwhelming.

Early racers had a huge rear spoiler.

1991 Carroll Shelby drives a prototype Viper as the pace car in the Indianapolis 500.

1992 The car goes on sale and proves a massive success. Chrysler has taken a huge risk building a car that costs nearly $60,000 and doesn't even have windows or air conditioning. It is a long-odds gamble that soon proves to be a winner for Chrysler.

1996 The GTS Coupe, first seen as a 'concept car' in 1993, finally goes on sale in Europe. Its chassis is stiffer and the engine and car are lighter, while the V10's power is increased to 450 bhp. The superior aerodynamics of the fixed hard top also help make it faster.

Sleek and fast: Viper GTS Coupe.

UNDER THE SKIN

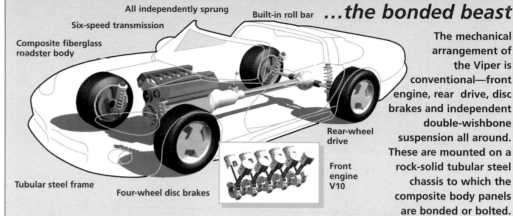

...the bonded beast

All independently sprung
Six-speed transmission
Built-in roll bar
Composite fiberglass roadster body
Rear-wheel drive
Front engine V10
Tubular steel frame
Four-wheel disc brakes

The mechanical arrangement of the Viper is conventional—front engine, rear drive, disc brakes and independent double-wishbone suspension all around. These are mounted on a rock-solid tubular steel chassis to which the composite body panels are bonded or bolted.

THE POWER PACK

...Outstanding V10 performance

The Viper is an outrageous sports car, so it makes sense that its power plant be equally impressive. During this time, Dodge was in ownership of Lamborghini, so it employed the Italian supercar company to develop an all-aluminum V10 mechanical masterpiece. Its sheer size of 488-cubic inches helps make 400 bhp and 488 lb-ft of torque for those made in 1992. By 1998, power was increase to 450 bhp.

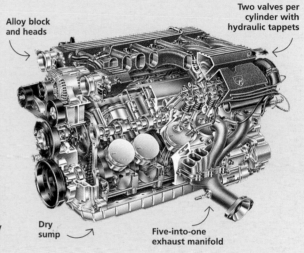

Alloy block and heads
Two valves per cylinder with hydraulic tappets
Dry sump
Five-into-one exhaust manifold

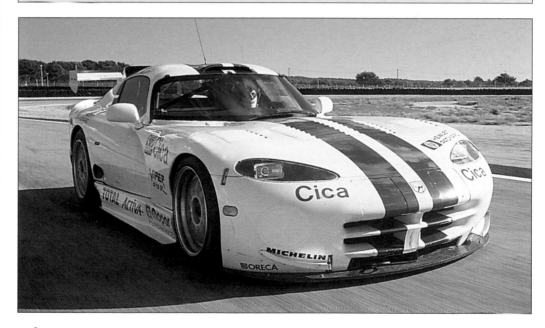

Viper Venom

As if the normal car wasn't powerful enough, John Hennessey has produced the Venom version with a staggering 550 bhp—150-bhp more than the original. It's enough to send a brave Viper driver to 100 mph in under 10 seconds and on to a top speed of 174 mph.

With 150-bhp extra bite, the Viper Venom is a car for the brave.

Dodge VIPER

The Viper's dramatic look of controlled aggression expresses the elemental power of its awesome V10 8-liter engine. It was styled by an in-house Chrysler design team led by Tom Gale.

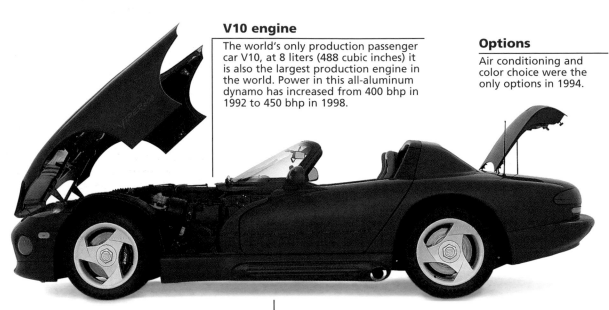

V10 engine

The world's only production passenger car V10, at 8 liters (488 cubic inches) it is also the largest production engine in the world. Power in this all-aluminum dynamo has increased from 400 bhp in 1992 to 450 bhp in 1998.

Options

Air conditioning and color choice were the only options in 1994.

Six-speed transmission

Borg-Warner six-speed transmission has an electronic shift lockout that automatically changes from 1st to 4th at light throttle.

Functional roll bar

Built-in roll bar stiffens body structure as well as adding protection. Removable rear window snaps into roll bar.

Limited slip differential

Limited slip differential helps to put the Viper's huge power down onto the road by reducing wheel spin.

Ellipsoidal headlights

Dodge describes the headlights on the Viper as Aero-Polyellipsoid. Behind those teardrop-shaped lenses are powerful halogen bulbs.

Tubular steel chassis

Steel tube chassis with steel cowl and sill structures; some composite body panels are bolted or bonded to the frame.

Unequal-sized tires

Different size tires and wheels front and rear help balance handling.

Exhaust air vents

The exaggerated cutaway sections in front of the doors form functional vents through which the hot engine compartment air is exhausted.

Plastic composite body

With a separate chassis, you would expect a fiberglass body, but the Viper uses more advanced plastic composite material with far greater damage resistance properties.

Specifications
1992 Dodge Viper RT/10

ENGINE

Type: V10, 90°

Construction: Aluminum heads and block with cast iron sleeves

Valve gear: Two valves per cylinders pushrods, roller hydraulic lifters

Bore and stroke: 4.0 in. x 3.9 in.

Displacement: 7,998 cc

Compression ratio: 9:1

Induction system: Multi-port electronic injection with ram tuning

Maximum power: 400 bhp at 4,600 rpm

Maximum torque: 488 lb-ft at 3,600 rpm

TRANSMISSION

Borg-Warner T-56 six-speed manual with electronic shift lock out

BODY/CHASSIS

Tubular steel chassis with two-seat fiberglass reinforced plastic convertible body

SPECIAL FEATURES

The six-speed transmission was specially designed to handle the immense torque.

The Viper is the only production car with a V10 engine.

RUNNING GEAR

Steering: Power-assisted rack-and-pinion

Front suspension: Unequal A-arms, anti-roll bar, coil springs, adjustable gas shocks

Rear suspension: Unequal A-arms, anti-roll bar, coil springs, toe-control links, adjustable gas shocks

Brakes: Brembo 13 in. vented disc with four-piston caliper (front); Brembo 13 in. vented disc with sliding caliper (rear)

Wheels: Alloy 10 in. x 17 in. (front), 13 in. x 17 in. (rear)

Tires: 275/40 ZR17 (front), 335/35 ZR17 (rear)

DIMENSIONS

Length: 175 in.   **Width:** 75.6 in.

Height: 44 in.   **Wheelbase:** 96.2 in.

Track: 59.5 in. (front), 60.6 in. (rear)

Weight: 3,477 lbs.

Ferrari **F355**

In creating the F355, Ferrari didn't just replace the old 348, it built a car so beautiful, so desirable and so fast that Ferrari customers almost stopped buying the awesome 12-cylinder Testarossa.

"...performance is astounding."

"There used to be a penalty to pay if you wanted supercar performance: the cars were big, heavy and awkward to drive. That's all changed with the F355. Its performance is astounding but, unlike some supercars, the F355 is a usable size, has a gear shifter that works easily, incredibly powerful brakes, and excellent, yet forgiving handling. If you're heavy-footed enough, you can break traction and get the tail out, but thankfully it's not too hard to get it back in a straight line."

The 355's cabin combines traditional Ferrari cues like a gated shifter with up-to-date stereo and air conditioning systems.

Milestones

1994 The F355 makes its sensational debut.

Dino was Ferrari's first small mid-engined car and the first of a long and successful line.

1994 When the motoring press gets their hands on a F355 it is instantly acclaimed as a classic and a far superior car to the previous 348 which—although much improved through its life—can never begin to match either the F355's visual or dynamic appeal.

348 is F355's immediate predecessor. It was the first of the line to have the V8 mounted longitudinally.

1995 The F355's appeal is broadened with the introduction of the most desirable of the range—the Spider. The fully convertible version supplements the existing Berlinetta hardtop coupe and the GTS with its removable targa-style roof.

UNDER THE SKIN

Italian styling

Pininfarina's alloy body panels cover a structure similar to the old 348: a chassis fabricated from sheet and tubular steel forming a central stress-bearing unit, with subframe at either end to carry suspension and engine. The V8 engine is mounted lengthwise behind the driver and double-wishbone suspension is used all around.

Four-wheel disc brakes

Pininfarina styling

Forty-valve, 3.5-liter V8

Longitudinally-mounted engine

THE POWER PACK

All-alloy construction

Four overhead camshafts

Five valves per cylinder

Titanium connecting rods

Forty-valve V8

The heart of any Ferrari is the engine. In this case there's an all-alloy 3.5-liter V8 with four overhead cams operating no fewer than five valves in each combustion chamber—three intake and two exhaust to give the most efficient breathing possible. No trick intake manifold or turbos are needed to extract an impressive 375 bhp at a heady 8,250 rpm. To cope with such high crankshaft speeds, the engine uses very strong titanium connecting rods.

Super Spider

The F355 range includes the desirable Berlinetta and GTS, but the pick of the bunch has to be the Spider. This convertible version offers almost unrivaled performance for an open-top car in a chassis which doesn't lose stiffness from having the roof removed.

F355 Spider is Ferrari's fastest convertible ever.

Ferrari **F355**

One of the many collaborations between Ferrari and Pininfarina has produced one of the greatest Ferraris. Its beautiful and balanced styling is coupled with stupendous performance from the 375-bhp V8 engine.

Limited luggage space

Like most mid-engined cars, the F355 has very limited space in the front luggage compartment.

Mid-mounted quad-cam engine

The quad-cam V8 engine is designed to rev very high, almost like a racing engine, and produces its excellent 375-bhp power output at a high 8,250 rpm. Even the maximum torque appears high up in the rev range at 6,000 rpm.

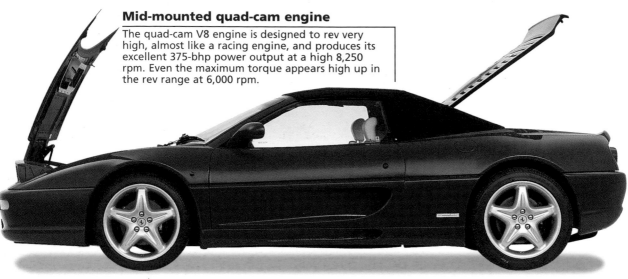

18-inch alloy wheels

Large, 18-inch magnesium-alloy wheels are used on the F355, in conjunction with ultra-low profile radial tires.

Active shocking

The F355 is equipped with sophisticated Bilstein shocks. Each has an electronically-controlled actuator which optimizes the shock setting within milliseconds.

Downforce aerodynamics

The F355 has a good drag coefficient, helped by the fact that it has a smooth, carefully designed underbody that also generates downforce at speed.

Power top

Pininfarina has designed convertibles for many companies, so it's no surprise that the convertible top on the F355 looks good.

Extra chassis stiffening

To make up for the lack of a roof, which adds a considerable amount to the strength and stiffness of any car, the F355's structure was cleverly strengthened without making the Spider any heavier than the Berlinetta.

Separate chassis

Ferraris are traditionally built with a separate chassis. The F355's is a mixture of tubular steel and sheet steel, folded and welded to form a very stiff structure.

Wishbone suspension

There was never any doubt what form of suspension the F355 would have. It could only be double wishbones at each corner, with coil springs and an anti-roll bar.

Specifications
1997 Ferrari F355 Spider

ENGINE
Type: V8
Construction: Light alloy block and heads
Valve gear: Five valves per cylinder operated by four belt-driven overhead camshafts
Bore and stroke: 3.35 in. x 3.03 in.
Displacement: 3,496 cc
Compression ratio: 11.0:1
Induction system: Bosch Motronic electronic injection
Maximum power: 375 bhp at 8,250 rpm
Maximum torque: 268 lb-ft at 6,000 rpm

TRANSMISSION
Six-speed manual

BODY/CHASSIS
Tubular and sheet steel central chassis with alloy two-door, two seat convertible body

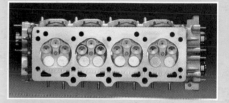

SPECIAL FEATURES
Fitting five valves to each cylinder improves efficiency, thus generating more power.

Underbody has aerodynamically designed undertray to achieve maximum ground effect.

RUNNING GEAR
Steering: Rack-and-pinion
Front suspension: Double wishbones, coil springs, adaptive shocks, anti-roll bar
Rear suspension: Double wishbones, coil springs, adaptive shocks, anti-roll bar
Brakes: Vented discs, 11.8 in. (front), 12.2 in. (rear), ABS
Wheels: Magnesium alloy, 7.5 in. x 18 in. (front), 10 in. x 18 in. (rear)
Tires: Michelin Pilot SX, 225/40 ZR18 (front), 265/40 ZR18 (rear)

DIMENSIONS
Length: 67.3 in. **Width:** 74.8 in.
Height: 46.1 in. **Wheelbase:** 96.5 in.
Track: 59.6 in. (front), 63.6 in. (rear)
Weight: 2,977 lbs.

Ferrari BOXER

When Ferrari transferred its Formula One know-how into a road car by using a flat-12 engine mounted behind the driver, it produced one of the most exciting of all the 1970s supercars, the Berlinetta Boxer.

"...for highly skilled drivers only."

"Generally recognized as one of the true Ferrari masterpieces, the Boxer has had an impressive record of achievement both on and off the track. At the limit, the Boxer is a car for highly skilled drivers only. The mid-engined flat 12 took Ferrari's reputation for handling to a new plane, but many teething problems remained—including a light front end. Still the Boxer is acknowledged decade after decade as one of the greats."

Ferrari's seat of power for the 1970s. The Boxer was the first road car to use a horizontally opposed 12-cylinder engine.

Milestones

1971 The first Berlinetta Boxer appears at the Turin Show, but isn't quite ready for production.

1973 Boxer production starts with the 365 GT4 BB. It uses a 4.4-liter flat-12 giving 360 bhp and an alleged top speed of 188 mph.

1976 To cope with increasing emission regulations which rob the engine of power, the displacement goes up to 4,942 cc to form the 512 BB. At 360 bhp, the claimed output is the same as the smaller engine's.

Le Mans Boxers of 1979 used this modified nose, but side vents presaged the Testarossa.

1981 The third and final version of the Boxer is the 512 BBi, the 'i' signifying that fuel injection has replaced carburetors. Power output was reduced to 340 bhp, but the torque spread is better and the wheels and tires are improved.

1984 The Boxer goes out of production to be replaced by the Testarossa which carries on the flat-12 theme.

UNDER THE SKIN

Traditional Ferrari

Although advanced in its mid-engine design, in other respects the Boxer is traditional with a separate and heavy steel chassis, although the engine is mounted in its own subframe. The suspension is also traditional with twin wishbones all around, and the heavy rear end has four coil spring/shock units.

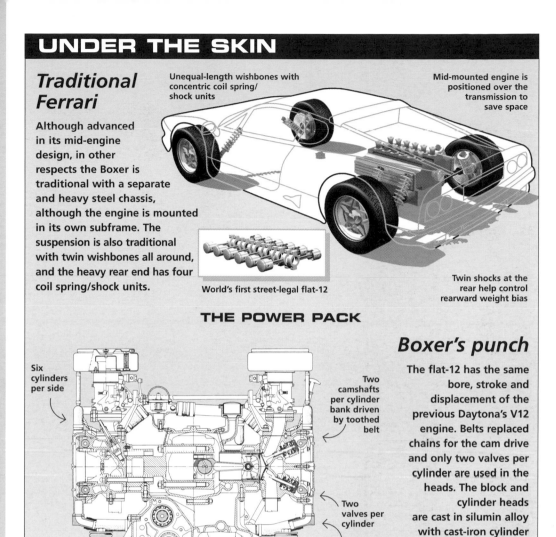

Unequal-length wishbones with concentric coil spring/shock units

Mid-mounted engine is positioned over the transmission to save space

World's first street-legal flat-12

Twin shocks at the rear help control rearward weight bias

THE POWER PACK

Six cylinders per side

Two camshafts per cylinder bank driven by toothed belt

Two valves per cylinder

Silumin light alloy block with alloy liners

Dry sump

Boxer's punch

The flat-12 has the same bore, stroke and displacement of the previous Daytona's V12 engine. Belts replaced chains for the cam drive and only two valves per cylinder are used in the heads. The block and cylinder heads are cast in silumin alloy with cast-iron cylinder liners shrunk into place. The crankshaft is machined from billet steel. Power output ranges from 340 to 360 bhp.

Le Mans Boxer

The first Boxer at Le Mans was the NART entry in 1975. With the 512 BB, the racing effort became more serious, with a series of lighter, 460-bhp cars racing in 1978. In '79, the BBs gained power (480 bhp) lost weight and got Pininfarina aerodynamic changes for Le Mans.

This Le Mans Boxer was driven by Pink Floyd's manager, Steve O' Rourke.

Ferrari BOXER

When Lamborghini beat Ferrari to the punch in making the first mid-engined supercar, Ferrari had to respond. The answer was the 365 GT4 BB, known to all simply as the Boxer.

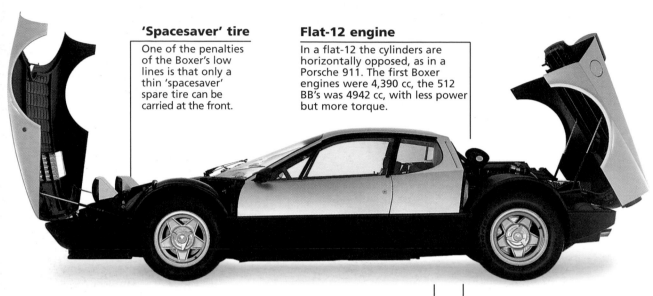

'Spacesaver' tire
One of the penalties of the Boxer's low lines is that only a thin 'spacesaver' spare tire can be carried at the front.

Flat-12 engine
In a flat-12 the cylinders are horizontally opposed, as in a Porsche 911. The first Boxer engines were 4,390 cc, the 512 BB's was 4942 cc, with less power but more torque.

Transmission below engine
With a long engine at the rear, mounted lengthwise, the only place to put the transmission was below the engine. This raised the engine, making the car's center of gravity higher than ideal.

Fiberglass body sections
Ferrari used fiberglass rather than steel for the lower body panels on the Boxer, a great help against rust which even Ferraris suffered from during this era.

Cooling ducts
One of the changes when the 512 BB was introduced was the addition of NACA-style cooling ducts to send cool air to the rear brakes.

Spoiler added to 512 BB

When the 512 BB was introduced a front spoiler was added to aid in high-speed stability.

Vented engine cover

Engine bay cooling is improved with the 512 BB with the use of this heavily slatted engine cover through which the hot air escapes.

Double spring/shock rear

To help control the weight of the large engine at the back, the Boxer's wishbone rear suspension has four coil spring/shock units.

Front radiator

Although the engine is behind the driver, the radiator stayed in the usual place in the front.

Specifications
1978 Ferrari Boxer

ENGINE
Type: Flat-12, quad-cam
Construction: Alloy cylinder block and cylinder heads
Valve gear: Two valves per cylinder operated by twin belt-driven overhead camshafts per bank of cylinder
Bore and stroke: 3.23 in. x 3.07 in.
Displacement: 4,942 cc
Compression ratio: 9.2:1
Maximum power: 360 bhp at 6,200 rpm
Maximum torque: 333 lb-ft at 4,600 rpm

TRANSMISSION
Five-speed manual

BODY/CHASSIS
Steel and fiberglass two-door, two-seat coupe with steel spaceframe and center steel monocoque chassis

SPECIAL FEATURES

Ferrari were the first to introduce a flat-12 engine in a road car.

Headlights only flip up when in use in order to increase aerodynamic efficiency.

RUNNING GEAR
Steering: Rack-and-pinion
Front suspension: Twin wishbones with coil springs, telescopic shocks and anti-roll bar
Rear suspension: Twin wishbones, two coil-spring/shock units per side and anti-roll bar
Brakes: Four-wheel discs, 11.3 in.
Wheels: Magnesium alloy 7.5 in. x 15 in. (front), 9 in. x 15 in. (rear)
Tires: 215/70VR15 (front), and 225/70VR15 (rear)

DIMENSIONS
Length: 173.2 in.   **Width:** 72 in.
Height: 44 in.   **Wheelbase:** 98.5 in.
Track: 57 in. (front), 61.5 in. (rear)
Weight: 3,427 lbs.

Ferrari **DAYTONA**

Until the arrival of the 550 Maranello, the Daytona was the last front-engined Ferrari supercar. Despite the old-fashioned layout, the Daytona is still one of the fastest supercars of all time.

"...meant to be driven hard."

"Ferrari made no compromises with the Daytona. It was meant to be driven fast and driven hard. At speed, the heavy unassisted steering—which makes parking a huge chore—lightens up. Drive the Daytona the way it was intended—hard—and it repays you. It seems to shrink around you and, despite its weight, it's agile and well behaved. You'll believe it was the fastest car of its time as it accelerates savagely long after other supercars have faded. The Daytona can easily go from 0-100 mph in just under 13 seconds."

The interior is classic Ferrari with a gated shifter and a steering wheel with a central Prancing Horse.

Milestones

1968 Ferrari unveils the 365 GTB/4 at the Paris Motor Show. The press calls it 'Daytona' in honor of Ferrari's success at the 1967 24-hour race. The name is unofficial, however, and never appears on the bodywork.

Daytona's predecessor was the 275 GTB, which also had a V12 engine.

1969 Production begins of both the coupe and convertible models. Ferrari also produces competition models. They have more power, with 400 bhp at 8,300 rpm and can reach more than 180 mph at tracks like Le Mans.

1971 Retractable headlights replace the original perspex-covered type.

1972 A competition Daytona wins its class at the 24 Hours of Le Mans, an achievement repeated in 1973 and 1974.

Daytonas took class victories at the 24 Hours of Le Mans in 1973 and 1974.

UNDER THE SKIN

Rear-mounted transmission

Separate chassis

Steel and alloy bodywork

Wishbone suspension all around

4.4-liter V12

Last of a kind

The Daytona is very traditional. Not only is it front-engined and rear-wheel driven, but the alloy and steel bodywork covers a multi-tube steel chassis, which is very sturdy and has no pretensions of saving weight. But with the transmission at the rear, weight distribution is perfect. Engine and transmission are connected by a hollow torque tube for the propshaft.

THE POWER PACK

V12 development

Nothing but a V12 would do for the Daytona and this is one of the best. Developed from the existing 275 GTB all-alloy, wet-liner engine, it has four instead of two camshafts. Driven by gears rather than chains it still has just two valves per cylinder. Six twin-choke carburetors were used to pour fuel directly and efficiently into each intake port. The car's official name, the 365 GTB/4, refers to capacity of each cylinder—365 cc.

Two valves per cylinder

Six twin-choke carburetors

Four chain-driven camshafts

Wet cylinder liners

Easy conversion

The rarest of the Daytonas is the Spyder. A little over 100 were built, although there are many fakes converted from the coupes. For factory and faker alike, the conversion was easy because the car has a strong separate chassis, so it does not rely on the roof for its strength.

Desirable and rare, the factory Spyder has often been copied.

Ferrari DAYTONA

The end of an era...but what a way to go! The combination of Pininfarina's perfectly proportioned body and a 4.4 liter Ferrari V12 makes it an instant classic, not to mention one of the world's fastest cars.

Quad-cam V12

The 365 GTB/4 model name helps explain the engine. The 365 stands for the size of each cylinder (which multiplied by the number of cylinders gives its 4.4 liter displacement).The 4 stands for the number of camshafts.

Rear-mounted transmission

The five-speed transmission shares the same alloy housing as the final drive. Because this is a two-seater with a short cabin, the length of gear linkage from the driver to the transmission is not excessive.

Engine air vents

After cool air has passed through the tiny front opening and through the V12's big radiator, it leaves the car via the two unobtrusive sunken vents in the hood.

Square-tube chassis

In the late-1960s, Ferrari was a very traditional manufacturer, so the Daytona's chassis is made up of many small-diameter square section tubes welded together. It is strong but heavy.

Front-to-rear torque tube

The engine and rear-mounted transmission are rigidly connected by a torque tube that houses the driveshaft.

Equal weight distribution

By setting the V12 back in the chassis and moving the transmission to the rear, Ferrari achieved a near-perfect 52/48 weight distribution without the complexity of a mid-engined car.

Wishbone suspension

Double wishbone suspension is fitted all around. To help the packaging, the rear spring/shock units are mounted above the top wishbone.

Alloy and steel body

The doors, hood and trunk lid are made of weight-saving alloy. The rest of the bodywork is steel.

1970 Ferrari 365 GTB/4 Daytona

ENGINE

Type: V12

Construction: Alloy block and heads with wet liners

Valve gear: Two valves per cylinder operated by four gear-driven overhead camshafts

Bore and stroke: 3.19 in. x 2.8 in.

Displacement: 4,390 cc

Compression ratio: 9.3:1

Induction system: Six Weber 40DCN 20 downdraft carburetors

Maximum power: 352 bhp at 7,500 rpm

Maximum torque: 330 lb-ft at 5,500 rpm

TRANSMISSION

Rear-mounted, five-speed manual

BODY/CHASSIS

Steel square tube separate chassis with alloy and steel two-door coupe or convertible body

SPECIAL FEATURES

Wrap-around front direction indicators were often mimicked after the Daytona's launch.

Four round tail lights and four exhausts tell you you've just been overtaken by a Daytona.

RUNNING GEAR

Steering: Recirculating ball

Front suspension: Double wishbones with coil springs, telescopic shocks and anti-roll bar

Rear suspension: Double wishbones with coil springs, telescopic shocks and anti-roll bar

Brakes: Vented discs, 11.3 in. dia. (front), 11.6 in. dia. (rear)

Wheels: Alloy, 7.5 in. x 15 in.

Tires: 215/7015

DIMENSIONS

Length: 174.2 in.   **Width:** 69.3 in.

Wheelbase: 94.5 in.   **Height:** 49 in.

Track: 56.7 in. (front), 56.1 in. (rear)

Weight: 3,530 lbs.

Ferrari DINO

One of Ferrari's best and most popular cars wasn't even officially called a Ferrari. Instead Ferrari's first mid-engined road car was named after Enzo's ill-fated son, Dino.

"...astounding cornering limits."

"The Dino 246 GT's quad-cam V6 is wonderful, flexible enough to putter around at low speeds but really sings from 3,500 rpm all the way to 7,800 rpm and will happily go way past the red line. It's matched to perfect gear ratios and a transmission that's better the faster you shift it. The mid-engined chassis and wishbones all around mean all the power is easily exploited. In its day, the Dino's cornering limits were astounding and they're still impressive today."

Although never badged as a Ferrari, the Dino interior has unmistakable cues like the gated shifter and large wood-rimmed, alloy-spoked steering wheel.

Milestones

1965 Coachbuilders Pininfarina build the Dino 206 GT Speciale for the Paris Motor Show with four round headlights in an extended nose.

1966 Pininfarina's next show car, the Dino, points the way to the production car, but its V6 engine is mounted longitudinally not transversely.

The Dino 206 Competizione: the last of Pininfarina's show cars.

1967 Definitive Dino 206 GT appears with no Ferrari badges on the Pininfarina stand at the Turin Motor Show.

1969 Engine is changed from an alloy to an iron block, and enlarged to 2.4-liters, while the body is made of steel rather than alloy. The 246 GT has a longer wheelbase than the 206.

1972 246 GT is joined by the GTS. The S stands for Spider or convertible, but it is really a Targa top with a removable roof panel.

Fiat, who built the engine, used it in their own Fiat Dino from 1966 to '75.

UNDER THE SKIN

Ferrari first

The Dino was advanced both in being mid-engined with its transverse V6 and in seeing Ferrari finally switching to rack-and-pinion steering. Otherwise, it is a traditional Ferrari with wishbone suspension and a tubular steel chassis onto which the body (made first in alloy and then in steel) is mounted. A central tunnel helped increase overall stiffness.

Steel body on later cars

Mid-engine transversely mounted

Tubular steel chassis

Wishbone suspension

Famous Ferrari V6

THE POWER PACK

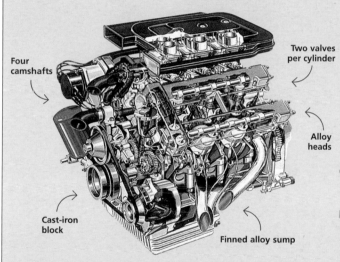

Four camshafts

Two valves per cylinder

Alloy heads

Cast-iron block

Finned alloy sump

Co-venture

The original 1,987-cc, alloy, quad-cam, wet-liner, 65-degree, 12-valve V6 was closely related to Ferrari's 1.6-liter Formula 2 engine. In 1969, the blocks were made from cast-iron to ease production (which was by Fiat rather than Ferrari). It was also given a larger, 2,418-cc, displacement with both a bigger bore and longer stroke. Power increased from 180 bhp to 195 bhp. Fiat also used the engine in both its original 2.0 and 2.4-liter forms in its front-engined Dino.

Dino 206

To the purist, the first Dino is the best. It has an alloy body rather than the steel body of the later 246. Its engine is made of alloy and closer to a racing motor than the later iron-block 2.4-liter V6. It is less powerful, but makes up for it by being lighter.

The classy yet strong 206 GT has a 2-liter engine and a light alloy body.

Ferrari DINO

The Dino did more than just combine a small race-bred quad-cam V6 in a beautiful lightweight alloy body—it was mid-engined and set new standards of handling for street-legal Ferrari sports cars.

Rear luggage compartment

The transverse engine means there is space behind it to carry luggage. All that will fit in the front is the spare wheel.

V6 quad-cam engine

By the time this 246 GT was produced, the engine block was made of iron. Ferrari shared the V6 engine with Fiat who used it in its own front-engined Dino.

Front-mounted radiator

Although there appears to be no room for it, the Dino's radiator is mounted in the nose, where it had to be angled to fit under the shallow nose.

Side air vents

Although the radiator is in the front, side air vents are still needed to feed air to the engine and oil cooler.

Alloy wheels

Ferrari used wire wheels from 1947 right up until the 1960s when alloys became standard.

Flying buttress design

Styling the back of a mid-engine car is difficult because it is necessary to leave access space. One solution is to have 'flying buttresses' where the line of the cabin is continued towards the rear of the car, but there's space between the two sides.

Vented disc brakes

Dinos have very effective vented disc brakes and they are the same size on all four wheels because the Dino's weight distribution is almost perfect.

Wishbone suspension

Like most high-performance cars, the Dino uses double wishbones with an anti-roll bar in the front and rear.

Steel bodywork

In 1969, Ferrari switched from alloy bodies to steel. That made the cars noticeably heavier than the original 206 GT but engine size and power were increased to compensate.

Specifications
1971 Ferrari Dino 246 GT

ENGINE
Type: V6
Construction: Cast-iron block and alloy cylinder heads
Valve gear: Two valves per cylinder operated by twin chain-driven overhead cams per bank of cylinders
Bore and stroke: 3.67 in. x 2.36 in.
Displacement: 2,418 cc
Compression ratio: 9.0:1
Induction system: Three Weber 40DCN carburetors
Maximum power: 195 bhp at 5,000 rpm
Maximum torque: 166 lb-ft at 5,500 rpm

TRANSMISSION
Five-speed manual

BODY/CHASSIS
Tubular steel chassis with steel two-door coupe body

SPECIAL FEATURES

Dino's simple door handles help leave the car's beautiful lines uncluttered.

Plastic headlight covers were popular with European manufacturers but became illegal in the U.S. and fell out of fashion.

RUNNING GEAR
Steering: Rack-and-pinion
Front suspension: Double wishbones, coil springs, telescopic shocks and anti-roll bar
Rear suspension: Double wishbones, coil springs, telescopic shocks and anti-roll bar
Brakes: Four-wheel vented discs, 10.6 in. dia.
Wheels: Cast alloy 6.5 in. x 14 in.
Tires: 205/70 VR14

DIMENSIONS
Length: 166.5 in.   **Width:** 67 in.
Height: 45 in.   **Wheelbase:** 92 in.
Track: 55.5 in. (front), 56 in. (rear)
Weight: 2,611 lbs.

Ferrari TESTAROSSA

If you could create lightning in the shape of a car, the result would be the Ferrari Testarossa 512. Grand Prix performance is only a throttle pedal away, delivered with an effortless rush of endless horsepower. Add the sensuous Pininfarina bodyshell and luxurious interior and you have the ultimate automotive dream.

"…blindingly fast."

"The first thing you notice is its outrageous low and wide profile set off by monstrous rear tires. The door sills are so wide, it's hard to climb in and there's little rear visibility. But this blood-red Testarossa has enough mystique for 10 cars, offers surprising civility, yet delivers stunning, endless power. Despite the quirky gated shifter, the clutch is light and the car moves effortlessly toward twice the speed limit. As a true Ferrari, it's exotic, refined and blindingly fast. No matter how fast you go, no matter what gear you're in, the Testarossa always seems to have more to come."

In the words of Ferrari's press department: "The cockpit: a living room at 190 mph."

Milestones

1964 Ferrari introduces the 512 F1, its first Grand Prix supercar with a flat-12 engine.

1976 Ferrari adopts the flat-12 concept for the road in the 512 BB. 'BB' stood for 'Berlinetta Boxer' (meaning a small sedan with a horizontally opposed engine). The Boxer packs a 340-bhp punch.

The Testarossa is in its element on the open road.

1984 The Testarossa is launched at the 1984 Paris Motor Show. Name means 'redhead,' describing the red painted cam covers. Sleeker than the 512 BB, the car is also more powerful (390 bhp) and faster (180 mph).

1992 With power up from 390 to 428 bhp, The 512 TR becomes Ferrari's luxury flagship. In Ferrari language, '512' means it has a displacement of five liters spread between 12 cylinders.

1994 With the 512 TR overshadowed by the new F355, Ferrari revamps the Testarossa, bringing out the 512 M with more performance and better looks.

1996 512 M production ends with the introduction of the front-engined 550 Maranello.

UNDER THE SKIN

Pininfarina styling

The 512 was built the way they used to build race cars, with aluminum body panels fixed to a tubular steel frame. But that's under the skin; on the outside it's a classic body design from Pininfarina, the Italian master, who worked with a wind tunnel to create a wind-cheating shape that stays glued to the road.

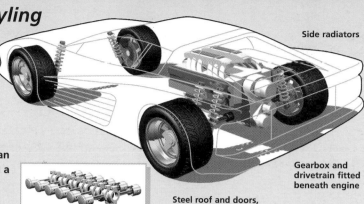

Side radiators

Gearbox and drivetrain fitted beneath engine

Steel roof and doors, aluminum body panels

Mid-mounted flat-12 engine

THE POWER PACK

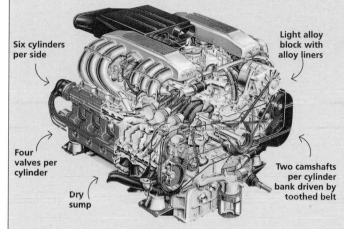

Six cylinders per side

Light alloy block with alloy liners

Four valves per cylinder

Two camshafts per cylinder bank driven by toothed belt

Dry sump

Flat-12 engine

Ferrari built its first flat-12 Grand Prix engine in 1964, and it put all it had learned on the track into this flat-12 for the street. The 5-liter motor of the Testarossa produces 390 bhp with an enormous torque output of 360 lb-ft at an accessible 4,500 rpm. It pushes the car to the mile in 38.3 seconds. Peak power comes at 6,750 rpm and the motor will spin to 7,250 rpm.

Last and best

The last of the Testarossa line was also the best. The 512 M of 1995, destined to be in production for only a couple of years, had its power boosted to 440 bhp. The final Testarossa model was much improved with updated and cleaner styling and more powerful brakes to help stop it from a claimed top speed of 195 mph.

The Testarossa shouts 'speed' even when it's stationary.

Ferrari TESTAROSSA

When a Testarossa roars down the street, all heads turn! The sheer beauty of Pininfarina's body styling, the unbridled power of the 390-bhp flat-12 and the luxurious ivory-leather interior makes this one of Maranello's masterpieces.

Side-mounted radiators

Behind the long, exposed ribs lies a fan-assisted radiator on each side of the car, angled to gain the maximum throughput of cooling air to the 5-liter engine.

Front-mounted battery

The battery is front-mounted, fractionally improving the rear-heavy weight distribution.

Five-spoke alloy wheels

Wheels are 16 inches in diameter (18 inches on the 512 TR) and the rear ones are a massive 10 inches wide.

Removable engine subframe

The rear subframe can be dropped out of the car complete with engine and gearbox to allow maximum access to the mechanics.

Gearbox under engine

With a flat-12 engine, the gearbox can be mounted under it without making the whole assembly too high. This keeps the overall length to a minimum.

Slatted rear lights

These are a deliberate echo of the car's most distinctive feature, the side strakes covering the radiator intakes.

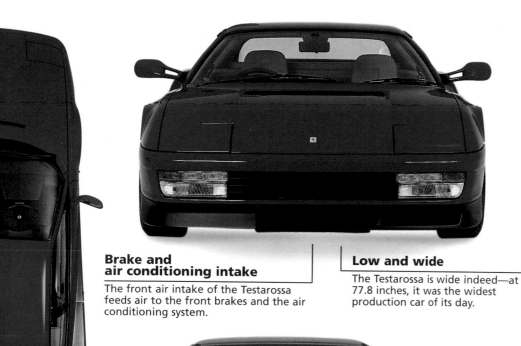

Brake and air conditioning intake

The front air intake of the Testarossa feeds air to the front brakes and the air conditioning system.

Low and wide

The Testarossa is wide indeed—at 77.8 inches, it was the widest production car of its day.

Wider rear track

To compensate for the rearward weight bias and the high center of gravity caused by the flat-12 engine, the rear track is an enormous 65.4 inches compared with the front track of 59.8 inches.

Luggage to the front

Because the engine is behind the driver, all the luggage has to fit in the front. Due to its odd shape, Ferrari supplied specially fitted leather luggage.

Huge front windshield

The shallow angle of the windshield produces a large area of glass—one reason why air conditioning is a standard Testarossa feature.

Specifications
1991 Ferrari Testarossa

ENGINE

Type: Flat-12
Construction: Light alloy block and heads
Valve gear: Four valves per cylinder, two belt-driven overhead camshafts per cylinder bank
Bore and stroke: 3.2 in. x 3.1 in.
Displacement: 4,942 cc
Compression ratio: 9.3:1
Induction system: Bosch KE-Jetronic electronic fuel injection
Maximum power: 390 bhp at 6,300 rpm
Maximum torque: 360 lb-ft at 4,500 rpm

TRANSMISSION

Five-speed manual with limited slip differential, mounted below engine

BODY/CHASSIS

Square-tube steel chassis with alloy and steel two-door supercar body

SPECIAL FEATURES

Distinctive side strakes feed air to the mid-mounted engine.

The 512 TR engine has greater power and improved flexibility, but still sounds magnificent.

RUNNING GEAR

Steering: Rack and pinion
Front suspension: Independent with double unequal-length wishbones, coil springs and shocks
Rear suspension: Independent with double unequal-length wishbones and twin coil spring/shock units per wheel
Brakes: Vented discs front and rear
Wheels: Alloy, 8 in. x 16 in. (front), 10 in. x 16 in. (rear)
Tires: 225/50 VR16 front, 255/50 VR16 rear

DIMENSIONS

Length: 176.7 in.
Width: 77.8 in.
Height: 44.5 in.   **Wheelbase:** 100.4 in.
Track: 59.8 in. (front), 65.4 in. (rear)
Weight: 3,675 lbs.

Ford **GT40**

The GT40 showed that when a company the size of Ford decides to go into racing, their vast resources will ensure success. After some initial teething trouble, the mighty V8 Ford humiliated the Ferraris with a sweep at Le Mans in 1966.

"...V8 thumps you in the back."

"Even in the road car, with its milder engine and rubber-bushed suspension it's easy to get a realistic impression of what it was like to drive the GT40s through the June heat at Le Mans. The open road and wide, sweeping corners soon beckon; somewhere you can floor the throttle and feel the gutsy V8 thump you in the back as it tears to 100 mph in just 12 seconds. If it's this good on the road, it must have been fantastic on the Mulsanne Straight."

The cabin is small and claustrophobic. Tall drivers cannot even fit in and miss out on one of the greatest driving experiences available.

Milestones

1963 After failing to buy Ferrari, Ford joins forces with Lola to turn the Lola GI into the prototype Ford GT.

1964 Now known as the GT40, the Ford makes its racing debut at the Nurburgring 1000 km. It is forced to retire, as it does in every race this year.

GT40 was so named because its overall height was 40 inches.

1965 Production starts for homologation and a GT40 wins its first race: the 2000-km Daytona Continental.

1966 The big-block cars finish 1-2-3 at Le Mans and win the International Sports Car Championship for GTs.

GT40 won Le Mans in 1968 and '69 after Ford had withdrawn from sports car racing in '67.

1967 Once again the car wins both the International Sports Car Championship and the 24 Hours of Le Mans. Although Ford withdraws from racing at the end of '67, the GT40 races on in the hands of the Gulf team, winning Le Mans again in '68 and '69.

UNDER THE SKIN

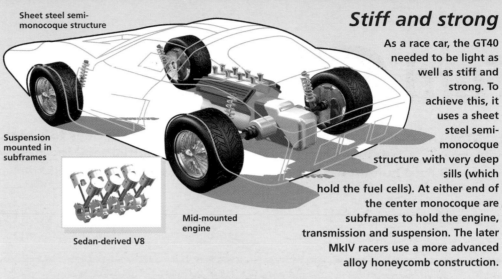

Sheet steel semi-monocoque structure

Suspension mounted in subframes

Sedan-derived V8

Mid-mounted engine

Stiff and strong

As a race car, the GT40 needed to be light as well as stiff and strong. To achieve this, it uses a sheet steel semi-monocoque structure with very deep sills (which hold the fuel cells). At either end of the center monocoque are subframes to hold the engine, transmission and suspension. The later MkIV racers use a more advanced alloy honeycomb construction.

THE POWER PACK

Tuning potential

Most GT40s used the 289-cubic inch V8 also found in the Sunbeam Tiger, Ford Mustang and early AC Cobra. With a cast-iron block and cylinder heads, a single camshaft operating two valves per cylinder via pushrods and rockers, it is not a sophisticated engine. Its design dates back to the 1950s, but it has huge tuning potential. In full racing tune, it can produce around 400 bhp which was more than enough to blow past the more sophisticated, but often less reliable, Ferraris.

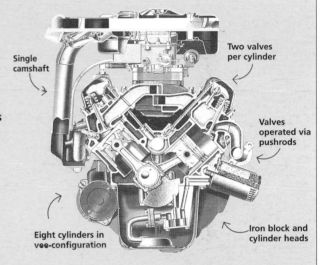

Single camshaft

Two valves per cylinder

Valves operated via pushrods

Eight cylinders in vee-configuration

Iron block and cylinder heads

Big blocks

Ford's first Le Mans-winning GT40 used the big-block 427-cubic inch engine; a unit that proved in the tough world of NASCAR racing it had the strength required for 24-hour racing. Only a few big-block cars were built.

Big-block cars had extra power and strength to compete in endurance racing.

Ford **GT40**

Fast and immensely strong, the GT40 showed what a production car company could do when it wanted to go racing, particularly with Carroll Shelby, father of the AC Cobra, running the racing program.

Final specification

Although this car first raced in 1965, it was later brought up to the final racing specs, those of the Le Mans-winning cars of 1968 and '69.

Mid-engined design

By the 1960s, it was obvious that a successful racing car had to be mid-engined and Ford followed suit. The engine is behind the driver, mounted lengthwise, and by 1968, the displacement of the small-block engine had risen to 302 cubic inches. With Gurney-Weslake-developed cylinder heads, as on this car, power output was up to 435 bhp.

Front-mounted radiator

Ford decided to keep the radiator in its conventional position rather than mounting it alongside or behind the engine as on some modern mid-engined designs.

Four-speed transmission

The first racers are equipped with a four-speed Colotti transmission with right-hand change. Road cars have a ZF five-speed box with conventional central shifter.

Opening side windows

GT40s get incredibly hot inside and although the main side windows do not open, there are small hinged windows to allow air to pass through the cockpit.

Fiberglass body

The GT40's body played no structural role, so it was made from fiberglass and consisted basically of two large hinged sections, which gave the best access during pit stops.

Radiator outlet

By 1968, the air passing through the radiator was exhausted through this one large vent. It has a small upturned lip on the leading edge to accelerate air flow through the radiator.

Competition record

This car was one of the first driven at Le Mans, in 1965 by Bob Bondurant, but it failed to finish after cylinder head gasket failure. Three years later, it came fourth in the 1000 km at Spa Francorchamps.

Magnesium suspension components

The GT40 is a heavyweight racing car, but some effort was still made to save weight—the magnesium suspension uprights, for example.

Halibrand wheels

The wide Halibrand wheels are made from magnesium, so they are very light. The design also provides good cooling for the disc brakes. They are a knock-off design for quick changes at pit stops.

M. COLVILL

Specifications
1967 Ford GT40 MkIII (road spec)

ENGINE

Type: V8
Construction: Cast-iron block and heads
Valve gear: Two valves per cylinder operated by single camshaft via pushrods and rockers
Bore and stroke: 4 in. x 2.87 in.
Displacement: 289 c.i.
Compression ratio: 10.5:1
Induction system: Single four-barrel Holley carburetor
Maximum power: 306 bhp at 6,000 rpm
Maximum torque: 328 lb-ft at 4,200 rpm

TRANSMISSION

Five-speed ZF manual transaxle

BODY/CHASSIS

Sheet steel central semi-monocoque with front and rear subframes and fiberglass two-door, two-seat GT body

SPECIAL FEATURES

The GT40 was made as low as possible to help its aerodynamics. On this car, to help fit a driver with helmet into the cockpit, this bump was added onto the roof.

To help achieve a low overall height, the exhaust pipes run over the top of the transmission.

RUNNING GEAR

Steering: Rack-and-pinion
Front suspension: Double wishbones with coil springs, telescopic shocks and anti-roll bar
Rear suspension: Trailing arms and wishbones with coil springs, telescopic shocks and anti-roll bar
Brakes: Discs, 11.5 in. dia. (front), 11.2 in. dia. (rear)
Wheels: Halibrand magnesium 6.5 in. x 15 in. (front), 8.5 in. x 15 in. (rear)
Tires: 5.5 in. x 15 in. (front), 7 in. x 15 in. (rear)

DIMENSIONS

Length: 169 in.   **Width:** 70 in.
Height: 40 in.   **Wheelbase:** 95.3 in.
Track: 55 in. (front), 53.5 in. (rear)
Weight: 2,200 lbs.

Ford MUSTANG GT

Although the Mustang enjoyed a performance renaissance during the 1980s, it did not have the same romance as the original. For 1994, an all-new retro-styled car arrived, which has become progressively more sophisticated.

"...truly refined performance."

"Compared to third-generation Mustangs, the current GT has much better ergonomics and feels tighter with no rattling or squeaking. The 4.6 liter modular V8, however, does not have as much torque and doesn't feel as fast as the 5.0-liter engine it replaced. Handling is noticeably better than the previous model and with much less understeer. Braking is excellent and safe, with standard ABS and four-wheel discs. The current 4.6 liter Mustang GT offers truly refined performance."

A twin-cowl dashboard layout is a retro touch which harks back to the original Mustang.

Milestones

1993 In the last month of the year the fourth-generation Mustang is launched in 3.8-liter V6 or 5.0-liter V8 forms, and in coupe or convertible body styles. The hatchback version is no longer offered.

Third-generation 5.0-liters were very powerful and had the same performance as 1960s muscle cars.

1994 The Mustang celebrates its 30th birthday and a 240-bhp Cobra version joins the range.

1995 A new modular 4.6-liter V8 engine arrives for 1996. All Mustangs receive new taillights and the GT gets revised 17-inch wheels.

The Mustang is heavily facelifted for 1999.

1998 Responding to criticisms of lack of power, the GT gets an additional 10 bhp. A standard value performance package is also offered to help boost flagging sales.

UNDER THE SKIN

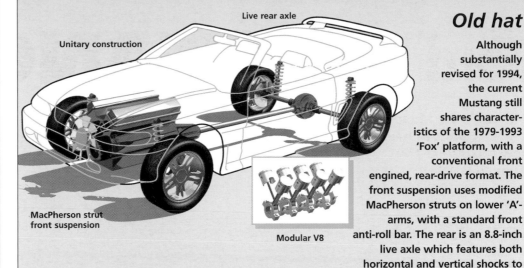

Live rear axle

Unitary construction

MacPherson strut front suspension

Modular V8

Old hat

Although substantially revised for 1994, the current Mustang still shares characteristics of the 1979-1993 'Fox' platform, with a conventional front engined, rear-drive format. The front suspension uses modified MacPherson struts on lower 'A'-arms, with a standard front anti-roll bar. The rear is an 8.8-inch live axle which features both horizontal and vertical shocks to reduce axle tramp.

THE POWER PACK

Modular-mania

Known as the SN95, the current Mustang's base engine is a 3.8-liter V6. Early fourth-generation GTs were powered by the venerable 5.0 liter V8, although for 1996 this was replaced by a version of Ford's overhead-cam 'Modular V8.' Displacing 4.6 liters, this engine has an alloy block and cylinder heads, with a single overhead cam layout and a composite intake manifold. In current trim it puts out the same power as the old 5.0-liter unit—225 bhp—but with slightly less torque.

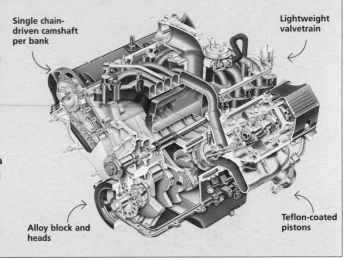

Single chain-driven camshaft per bank

Lightweight valvetrain

Alloy block and heads

Teflon-coated pistons

Five liter

Although the 4.6 is undeniably sophisticated, many prefer the 1994- 1995 5.0-liter cars. The old pushrod V8 is still satisfying and simpler to maintain. Best of all, there is an abundance of speed equipment to make these cars go even faster.

Many enthusiasts prefer the older 5.0-liter Mustangs.

Ford MUSTANG GT

The GT was essentially a sport appearance package on the original Mustang and, since 1982, has been the mainstream performance variant. Current GTs are often loaded with options, although they still offer plenty of power.

Choice of body styles

Current Mustangs come in either two-door coupe or convertible forms. In the interests of torsional rigidity, the hatchback style, as seen on the 1979–1993 model, was discontinued.

Modern V8 engine

The Mustang underwent something of a revolution in 1996 when the old pushrod V8 was replaced by a modern overhead-cam unit. The engine, although smaller in displacement (4.6 liters versus 5.0 liters), comes close to duplicating the power of the 5.0 liter engine it replaces.

Luxury equipment

Cruise control, twin airbags, air-conditioning, tilt steering and foglights are popular optional equipment. Power windows, door locks, mirrors and lumbar support are all standard on the Mustang GT.

Quadrashock rear suspension

Since 1985, all factory V8-powered Mustangs have had an extra pair of rear shocks, mounted horizontally, to reduce axle wind-up under hard, standing-start acceleration.

Retro-styling

When Ford consulted enthusiasts on how the fourth-generation Mustang should look, many wanted a return to the original 1965. Thus, the current car features retro touches such as side scoops and triple taillights and the pony emblem in the grill. However, it remains contemporary and aerodynamically efficient.

Four-wheel disc brakes

Braking was always a problem on late third-generation cars. However, the current Mustang is fitted with four-wheel ABS-assisted disc brakes which are a tremendous improvement.

Five-speed transmission

All Mustangs can be ordered with the Borg-Warner T-45 five-speed manual transmission, with two sets of final-drive ratios: 2.73 or 3.08:1. Many buyers specify the optional 4R70W four-speed automatic, which is remarkably refined.

Specifications

1998 Ford Mustang GT

ENGINE

Type: V8

Construction: Alloy block and heads

Valve gear: Two valves per cylinder operated by a single overhead camshaft per bank

Bore and stroke: 3.60 in. x 3.60 in.

Displacement: 4.6 liter

Compression ratio: 9.0:1

Induction system: Sequential electronic fuel injection

Maximum power: 225 bhp at 4,400 rpm

Maximum torque: 285 lb-ft at 3,500 rpm

TRANSMISSION

Borg-Warner T-45 five-speed manual

BODY/CHASSIS

Integral chassis with two-door steel convertible body

SPECIAL FEATURES

A strut tower brace helps to improve body stiffness.

A large rear spoiler is standard with the Mustang GT package.

RUNNING GEAR

Steering: Rack-and-pinion

Front suspension: MacPherson struts with coil springs and shock absorbers

Rear suspension: Live axle with coil springs and quad shock absorbers

Brakes: Discs (front and rear)

Wheels: Alloy, 17-in. dia.

Tires: Goodyear Eagle 245/45 ZR17

DIMENSIONS

Length: 181.5 in. **Width:** 71.5 in.

Height: 53.0 in. **Wheelbase:** 101.2 in.

Track: 60.0 in. (front), 58.6 in. (rear)

Weight: 3,462 lbs.

Acura **NSX**

Honda's mission was to build the perfect sports car. The result was Japan's first supercar, the stunning 274-bhp Acura NSX. From nowhere, Honda had joined battle with Ferrari.

"...simply amazing."

"It's quite simply the easiest supercar in the world to drive fast. There are no tricks up its sleeve, no quirks to learn. You adapt to the car in minutes and can then just enjoy everything about it. The engine has power everywhere, revs to over 7,000 rpm in an instant, and sounds wonderful. The NSX is a great mix of comfort and power that few cars can equal. Its combination of ride, handling, and road-holding ability is simply amazing."

NSX interior is typically Japanese—functional if not stylish. Fully automatic transmission was replaced by the dated F-matic semi-automatic.

Milestones

1984 Honda's NSX project (which stands for New Sports car eXperimental) gets underway.

1989 NSX debuts at the Geneva Auto Show.

The clean good looks of NSX have not dated.

1990 Production begins in September at a new factory at Tochigi, north of Tokyo. Built specifically for the NSX, Tochigi produces 25 cars a day but that figure soon increases. The production car is only 88 lbs. heavier than the show car with a wheelbase that is 1.2 inches longer.

1994 Minor revisions are made to the NSX by giving it wider, lower-profile tires—215/45ZR16 at the front and 245/40ZR17 at the rear—with the rear wheels now increased to 17-inches in diameter.

1995 Targa top NSX T version is introduced with removable top. F-matic semi-automatic transmission is introduced to allow push-button shifting. Electric power-assisted steering is used on the manual as well as the automatic version.

UNDER THE SKIN

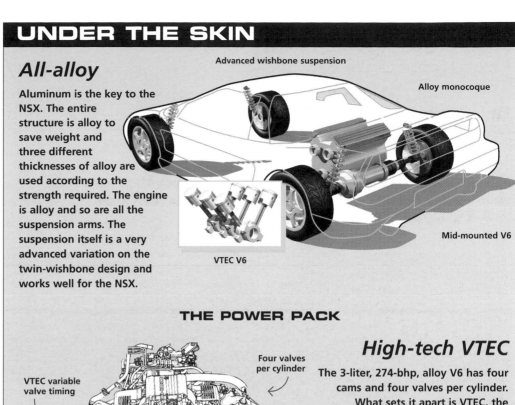

Advanced wishbone suspension

Alloy monocoque

Mid-mounted V6

VTEC V6

All-alloy

Aluminum is the key to the NSX. The entire structure is alloy to save weight and three different thicknesses of alloy are used according to the strength required. The engine is alloy and so are all the suspension arms. The suspension itself is a very advanced variation on the twin-wishbone design and works well for the NSX.

THE POWER PACK

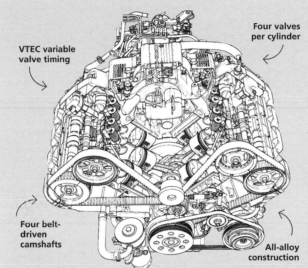

VTEC variable valve timing

Four valves per cylinder

Four belt-driven camshafts

All-alloy construction

High-tech VTEC

The 3-liter, 274-bhp, alloy V6 has four cams and four valves per cylinder. What sets it apart is VTEC, the variable valve timing device, which makes the engine perform even better at high rpm by introducing wilder camshaft timing, while sacrificing nothing on the bottom end where the torque is maximized. Features like titanium connecting rods mean the V6 can rev safely to 8,000 rpm and maximum power is produced at a high 7,000 rpm. The engine has a direct ignition system with an individual coil for each cylinder.

Class winner

With relatively few changes, the NSX made an effective GT racing car. In 1995 a privately-entered Japanese car won the GT2 class at the 24 Hours of Le Mans and finished 8th overall. The NSX had an average speed of 97 mph for the 24-hour race.

NSX won GT2 class in the 1995 24 hours of Le Mans.

Acura NSX

Fast, red, and low—surely it was a new Ferrari? Hard to believe, but it was built by Honda. The NSX was technically more advanced than its Ferrari opposition when it was launched in 1990.

Panoramic vision

Many supercars are very hard to see out of, but not the NSX. Out of the maximum 360 degrees which would be complete all-round vision, the Acura driver can see through 312.

Aluminum monocoque

Now a few makers, like Audi, are following Honda's lead in making all the car's structure in alloy rather than steel. In the NSX, 309 lbs. is saved with no loss of strength.

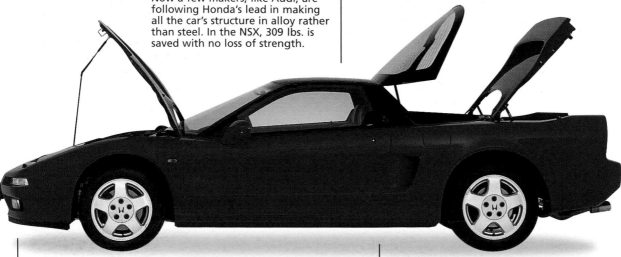

Fly-by-wire throttle

In the latest cars there's no mechanical link between the throttle and the engine. An electronic link relays the position of the throttle and the rate at which it's being pressed. The driver can't tell the difference.

Rear weight bias

The NSX is a mid-engined car but the weight is actually biased slightly to the rear—58 percent of the weight is on the rear wheels.

Double-glazed window

Between the driver and the mid-mounted engine there's a double-glazed panel which works well in suppressing the noise. The double glazing also means it never mists up.

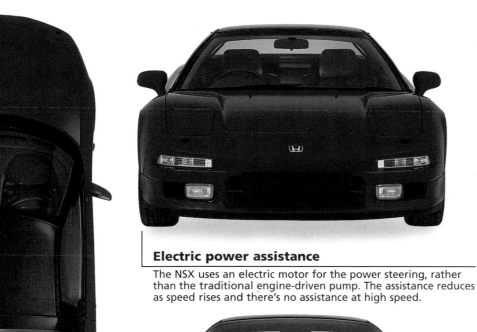

Electric power assistance

The NSX uses an electric motor for the power steering, rather than the traditional engine-driven pump. The assistance reduces as speed rises and there's no assistance at high speed.

Larger rear tires

The NSX started life with 16-inch rear wheels and 15-inch fronts. In 1994 that changed to 16-inch and 17-inch wheels with 215/45 ZR16 tires at the front and 245/40 ZR17s at the rear.

Aerodynamic design

A very low coefficient of drag with a smooth underside reduces turbulence. The car also has resistance to side winds and the whole rear section of the car, not just the wing, is designed to reduce lift.

Specifications
1993 Acura NSX

ENGINE
Type: V6 quad cam
Construction: Alloy block and heads
Valve gear: Four valves per cylinder operated by four belt-driven overhead cams with VTEC variable valve timing
Bore and stroke: 3.54 in. x 3.07 in.
Displacement: 2,977 cc
Compression ratio: 10.2:1
Induction system: Honda electronic fuel injection
Maximum power: 274 bhp at 7,000 rpm
Maximum torque: 210 lb-ft at 5,300 rpm

TRANSMISSION
Five-speed manual

BODY/CHASSIS
Alloy two-door, two-seat coupe with alloy monocoque chassis

SPECIAL FEATURES

VTEC cams have three lobes per pair of valves. At low rpm the center lobe is inoperative but beyond 5,800 rpm it comes into operation to give more, and longer, valve opening, resulting in more power.

Alloy monocoque is light and immensely strong and stiff.

RUNNING GEAR
Steering: Rack-and-pinion
Front suspension: Double wishbones, coil springs, telescopic shocks and anti-roll bar
Rear suspension: Double wishbones with coil springs, telescopic shocks and anti-roll bar
Brakes: Vented discs front and rear, 11.1 in. dia. Honda ABS
Wheels: Alloy 6.5 in. x 15 in. (front), 8 in. x 16 in. (rear)
Tires: 205/50ZR15 (front), 225/50ZR16 (rear)

DIMENSIONS
Length: 173.4 in.   **Width:** 71.3 in.
Height: 46.1 in.
Track: 59.4 in. (front), 60.2 in. (rear)
Weight: 3,021 lbs.

Jaguar E-TYPE

The E-type appeared like something from outer space in 1961. Nothing else at the price could compete with its combination of great beauty and amazing performance. It remains one of the all-time great sports cars.

"...the thrill of a lifetime."

"A combination of narrow bias-ply tires, 265 bhp and a 150 mph top speed sounds like a real challenge, but the E-type is a joy to drive. The view down the never-ending hood promises the thrill of a lifetime and that's just what the E-type delivers. Power flows smoothly from the superb straight-six engine and flooring the throttle, even at 100 mph, makes the nose rise as the car surges forward toward the 150 mph mark."

Simple but stylish—the E-type's dashboard is stocked with all the necessary gauges for a sports car.

Milestones

1961 Orders flood in
for the new Jaguar E-type, following its launch at the Geneva Motor Show.

1964 An enlarged,
4.2-liter engine is installed, giving more torque, but similar performance. An improved transmission is introduced.

The series was extended with addition of 2+2 with occasional rear seats.

1966 The larger 2+2
coupe, with small rear seats and a raised roofline is launched.

1968 Series II models have larger hood opening, more prominent front and rear lights and unfaired headlights.

Series III cars have V12 engine and a more prominent grill.

1971 A new 272 bhp,
5.3-liter alloy V12 is installed to form the Series III Roadster and Coupe 2+2 (the two-seater coupe is dropped). These have flared wheel arches and bolder radiator grills. It has a top speed of more than 145 mph.

1975 Production ends after 72,507 have been built.

UNDER THE SKIN

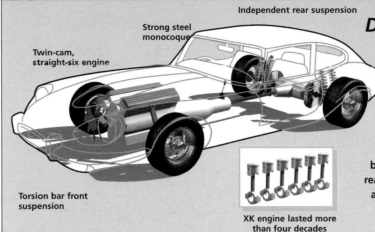

Independent rear suspension

Strong steel monocoque

Twin-cam, straight-six engine

Torsion bar front suspension

XK engine lasted more than four decades

D-type inspired

The E-type's construction was advanced, with a central monocoque inspired by the racing D-type Jaguars. A square-section tube frame carries the engine and front suspension and is bolted to the bulkhead. The rear suspension, mounted on a separate subframe, is also advanced with wishbones and double shock units while the driveshafts also act as suspension arms.

THE POWER PACK

Long-lived XK

One of the most famous and strong engines of all time powered the E-type. The XK straight-six twin-cam was developed during and after the war and first appeared in the successful XK120 sports car in 1948. As well as being installed on most of Jaguar's postwar cars, it also powered the all-conquering C- and D-types to victory at Le Mans. In fact, Jaguar continued to use the XK engine until 1992, when production of the 24-year-old Daimler DS420 limousine finally ended.

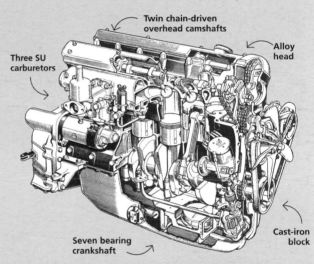

Twin chain-driven overhead camshafts

Alloy head

Three SU carburetors

Seven bearing crankshaft

Cast-iron block

Aluminum E-type

In 1963, Jaguar built a small series of Lightweight E-types. They had aluminum monocoque and body panels rather than steel and also alloy block engines to save weight. Despite producing between 320 and 344 bhp from their highly developed fuel-injected engines, they were outclassed on the track by Ferrari's 250 GTO.

Only 12 of the aluminum-bodied Lightweights were built.

Jaguar E-TYPE

It is no surprise the Jaguar E-type is sleek—it is the work of aero-dynamicist Malcolm Sayer, with the usual input from Jaguar boss, William Lyons, himself one of the greatest English car stylists.

Short wheelbase

Although the E-type appears to be long and sleek, its wheelbase is actually shorter than those of the Jaguar XK120, 140 and 150 sports cars that came before it.

Front-hinged hood

To allow easy access to the E-type's long, straight-six engine for maintenance and repairs, the whole hood hinges forward.

Torsion bar front suspension

A classic double-wishbone setup is used for the front suspension, sprung by torsion bars running lengthwise rather than the more usual coil springs, which would take up more underhood space.

Knock-off wheels

Wire spoke wheels with knock-off hubs are standard equipment on the early E-type. When the Series II was launched, chrome steel disc wheels became available.

Independent rear suspension

Jaguar's first car to have independent suspension was the E-type. The complete assembly is encapsulated in a separate subframe, which is attached to the monocoque via bonded rubber mountings to reduce noise transference.

Semi-monocoque construction

The E-type was built around a very strong and rigid central monocoque of sheet steel rather than on a separate chassis like some of its rivals.

Faired-in headlights

To make the E-type even more aerodynamic, the headlights on the early cars have perspex covers, later removed due to changing Federal regulations in the U.S.

Louvered hood

E-types generate a lot of heat under the low hood, which escapes through 14 rows of louvers on the hood.

Inboard rear brakes

Not only does the E-type boast disc brakes all around, but they are mounted inboard at the rear, reducing unsprung weight and giving the suspension less work.

Specifications

1961 Jaguar E-Type Roadster

ENGINE

Type: Straight-six twin-cam

Construction: Cast-iron block and alloy cylinder head

Valve gear: Two valves per cylinder operated by twin chain-driven overhead camshafts

Bore and stroke: 3.43 in. x 4.17 in.

Displacement: 3,781 cc

Compression ratio: 9.0:1

Induction system: Three SU carburetors

Maximum power: 265 bhp at 5,500 rpm

Maximum torque: 260 lb-ft at 4,000 rpm

TRANSMISSION

Four-speed manual

BODY/CHASSIS

Steel two-seat convertible with center steel monocoque chassis and front and rear subframes

SPECIAL FEATURES

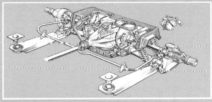

The advanced independent rear suspension can be removed complete from the car in its own separate subframe.

Shallow and wide windshield needs three short wipers to keep it clear.

RUNNING GEAR

Steering: Rack-and-pinion

Front suspension: Double wishbones with longitudinal torsion bars, shocks and anti-roll bar

Rear suspension: Lower wishbones with driveshafts as upper links and twin coil spring/shock units per side

Brakes: Discs all around, inboard at rear

Wheels: Wire spoked 5 in. x 15 in.

Tires: Dunlop 6.40 x 15 RS5 bias-plies

DIMENSIONS

Length: 175.5 in.   **Width:** 165.3 in.

Height: 48 in.   **Wheelbase:** 96 in.

Track: 50 in. (front and rear)

Weight: 2,463 lbs.

Jaguar XK8

The new V8-engined XK8 has gloriously recaptured the beauty, the style, and the performance forever associated with the legendary E-type. It's much more of a sports car than its XJS predecessor.

"...drives as good as it looks."

"The XK8 drives as good as it looks. It has all the Jaguar hallmarks; it's smooth, incredibly refined, and has a fantastic ride that can deal with the worst mid-corner bumps. The previous unresponsive automatic transmission from the XJS has been replaced by a new five-speed automatic unit. It's matched to an improved overhead cam V8 engine that can take the XK8 past 150 mph. The chassis is well balanced, although the steering is light."

In the XK8, you're in the lap of luxury with wood and leather everywhere.

Milestones

1975 E-type is replaced by the XJS, in coupe form only.

1978 Pininfarina displays its idea of a convertible version of the XJS. Based on the V12 XJS, the Spider is highly acclaimed. Its smooth flowing lines influence the XK8's design for more than 20 years.

XJS was distinctive but could never be described as beautiful the way the E-type was.

Almost 20 years ago, Pininfarina showed the way forward with this smooth-flowing design study.

1993 The program to build the XK8 is approved.

1996 The XK8 makes its debut at the Geneva Show in Europe and its all-important American debut at the New York Show. American sales are expected to run at 60 percent of total production; and 70 percent of those are expected to be convertibles, and only 30 percent coupes.

UNDER THE SKIN

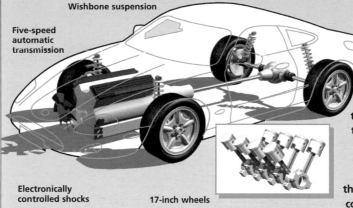

Wishbone suspension

Five-speed automatic transmission

Electronically controlled shocks

17-inch wheels

Jaguar's first V8

Wishbone suspension

The XK8 is a classically simple design with the engine mounted at the front, driving the rear wheels through a five-speed automatic transmission. Double wishbone suspension is used for all four wheels. To give the handling precision lacking in the XJS, there's a stiff front cross member connecting the front suspension on each side.

THE POWER PACK

Jaguar's new V8

The 290-bhp 4-liter V8 is only Jaguar's fourth completely new engine and the first V8. It's the lightest in its class, an all-alloy design that has Nikasil-plated bores instead of liners. Four overhead camshafts control four valves per cylinder. Intake camshaft timing can be changed electronically and each spark plug has its own ignition coil. The timing for each cylinder is precisely controlled by the engine management system. Most of the engine's 290 lb-ft of torque is available from 1,400 to 6,400 rpm.

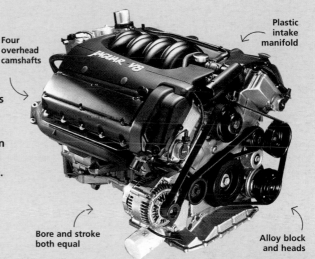

Four overhead camshafts

Plastic intake manifold

Bore and stroke both equal

Alloy block and heads

U.S. bound

In the right climate, the Jaguar XJ8 to buy has to be the convertible—even though it costs an extra $5,000. At any speed up to 10 mph, one touch of the switch will raise or lower the power top in less than 20 seconds, and doesn't sacrifice any trunk space.

To preserve trunk space, the convertible's top does not fold away completely.

Jaguar **XK8**

Styled to bring back sports-car excitement to the Jaguar range, the XK8 offers two of its traditional virtues—grace and pace— although it lacks much usable space in the back.

Wishbone suspension

Double-wishbone suspension is used for all four wheels to give the optimum wheel control and the best possible handling.

New V8 engine

Jaguar's new 4-liter V8 is light but rigid, making it refined as well as powerful. The quad-cam 32-valve V8 is tuned to give 80 percent of its torque over a wide range, making the car easy to drive.

Air conditioning

Naturally, the coupe has standard air conditioning, but so does the convertible.

CATS sport package

Optional Computer Active Technology Suspension (CATS) with larger, 18-inch alloy wheels, unidirectional front tires, and firmer suspension settings are available on the coupe.

Sophisticated security

Each Jaguar XK8 ignition key is electronically coded and unique. Alpha dots—microscope particles with the vehicle's identification number—are concealed in the car.

Anti-lock brakes

Large four-wheel vented discs brakes give the XK8 very impressive stopping power, but to make it even safer, anti-lock braking is standard equipment, along with traction control.

Electronically controlled shocks

For European-spec cars, the ACD (Active Controlled Damping) gives increased stability in varying road surfaces and braking conditions, each wheel's shock automatically adjusting to suit the conditions.

Advanced construction

The steel body is made from the minimum number of pressings, reducing the amount of joints and increasing strength.

Specifications
1997 Jaguar XK8

ENGINE

Type: V8

Construction: Light alloy block and heads

Valve gear: Four valves per cylinder operated by four belt-driven overhead camshafts

Bore and stroke: 3.38 in. x 3.38 in.

Displacement: 3,996 cc

Compression ratio: 10.75:1

Induction system: Electronic fuel injection

Maximum power: 290 bhp at 6,100 rpm

Maximum torque: 290 lb-ft at 4,250 rpm

TRANSMISSION

Five-speed automatic

BODY/CHASSIS

Unitary steel with two-door, 2+2 coupe body

SPECIAL FEATURES

With a five-speed automatic transmission manually selecting the gears can be confusing, but Jaguar's unique J gate sorts out that problem. Gear positions 2, 3 and 4 are on one side of the gate, so it's impossible to get confused with the other gears.

Front styling deliberately harks back to the look of the E-type.

RUNNING GEAR

Steering: Power-assisted rack-and-pinion

Front suspension: Double wishbones with coil springs, telescopic shocks and anti-roll bar

Rear suspension: Double wishbones, coil springs, telescopic shocks and anti-roll bar

Brakes: Vented four-wheel discs, with standard ABS

Wheels: Alloy, 8 in. x 17 in.

Tires: 245/50 ZR17

DIMENSIONS

Length: 187.4 in. **Width:** 79.3 in.

Height: 51 in. **Wheelbase:** 101.9 in.

Track: 59.2 in. (front), 59 in. (rear)

Weight: 3,763 lbs.

Lamborghini COUNTACH

Ferruccio Lamborghini liked to keep Ferrari on its toes. First he beat Ferrari into production with the mid-engined Miura, then he produced one of the world's most outrageous, and fastest, supercars—the Countach. During the 1970s and 1980s, it became the supercar to have.

"...acceleration is superb."

"Once you've made your way past the wide sills, the Countach is a revelation; forward visibility is exceptionally good, even if everything behind is a mystery. Then again, no one is going to be overtaking you in a Countach. The clutch is heavier than you expect and the dog-leg first gear takes some mastering. Its acceleration is superb and matched by phenomenal grip, excellent brakes, perfect steering and handling with no hidden vices."

The cockpit is simple, clean and at your command. However, the dog-leg first gear can be a little tricky.

1971 Bertone-styled Countach is unveiled at the Geneva Motor Show.

Early models had the purest lines of all, but still looked dramatic.

1974 Countach goes into production as the LP400 with a 375-bhp 4-liter V12 and a top speed of 190 mph.

1978 Improvements and a switch to the new low-profile Pirelli P7 tires bring a new model name: LP400S.

1982 Engine is stretched to 4.8 liters to form the LP500S.

1985 Another engine stretch, to 5.2 liters, and a switch to four valves per cylinder results in the powerful Quattrovalvole, with 455 bhp.

1988 Anniversary model, a QV with minor restyling, is the final Countach which lasts until 1991 when the Diablo comes into production.

1980s LP500S radiate power, aggression, and speed.

UNDER THE SKIN

Old and new

The chassis is as old fashioned as the body styling was futuristic. A complicated network of round steel tubes are welded together to form a complicated, but immensely strong spaceframe chassis. Much of its strength comes from the two massive fabricated sill sections. A light steel tube superstructure holds the alloy body which is welded, riveted, or bonded in place.

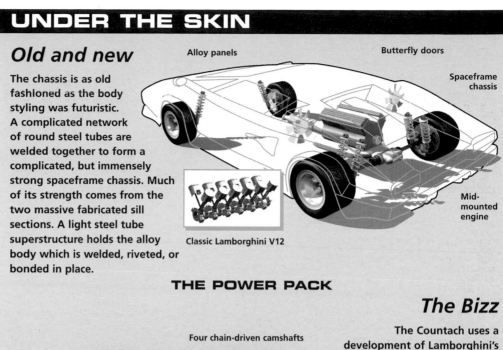

Alloy panels

Butterfly doors

Spaceframe chassis

Mid-mounted engine

Classic Lamborghini V12

THE POWER PACK

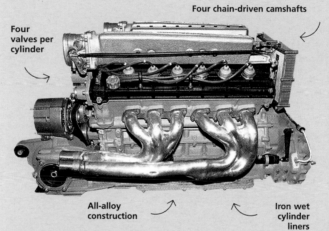

Four chain-driven camshafts

Four valves per cylinder

All-alloy construction

Iron wet cylinder liners

The Bizz

The Countach uses a development of Lamborghini's first V12 designed by ex-Ferrari engineer Giotto Bizzarrini. The all-alloy 60-degree engine has four chain-driven overhead cams and the pistons run in iron wet liners. At first it was four liters and 375 bhp, then grew to 4.8 and 5.2 liters. It was given four valves per cylinder in 1985 which helped boost power to 455 bhp. Quattrovalvoles use carburetors in Europe, but fuel injection is used on cars exported to the U.S.

Happy anniversary

The Countach's looks are very dramatic, and the most outrageous of all were the last cars, the 1988 Anniversary model. These have straked skirts and extended wheel arches, which first came with the LP400S in 1978 to cover its huge alloy wheels. Power came from the standard Quattrovalvoles engine.

Even in standard form, the Anniversary model was outrageous.

Lamborghini COUNTACH

Design a car as dramatic as the Countach and you just have to make it perform the way it looks. It looked like the fastest car in the world and Lamborghini made sure it was.

Mid-mounted V12

The long V12 engine is mounted lengthwise with the transmission ahead of the engine. It was a change from Lamborghini's previous supercar, the Miura, which has its V12 engine mounted transversely.

Upright opening doors

Lamborghini could have made the Countach's doors open in the normal way, but that would have had nothing like the dramatic impact of doors that opened straight up, each supported on a single gas strut.

Radiator ducts

Air flows into the huge ducts and electric fans blow the cool air across the side-mounted radiators.

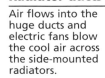

Split-rim alloy wheels

The circle of tiny bolts around each wheel shows that the Countach runs on split-rim alloys. The difference in size between front and rear wheels is enormous: the rears are 12-inches wide and the fronts 8.5 inches.

Flared wheel arches

The original Countach had no wheel-arch flares. They had to be added in 1978 when larger wheels and wider tires were fitted.

Optional rear wing

This car does without the optional rear wing which is as much for style as aerodynamic effect.

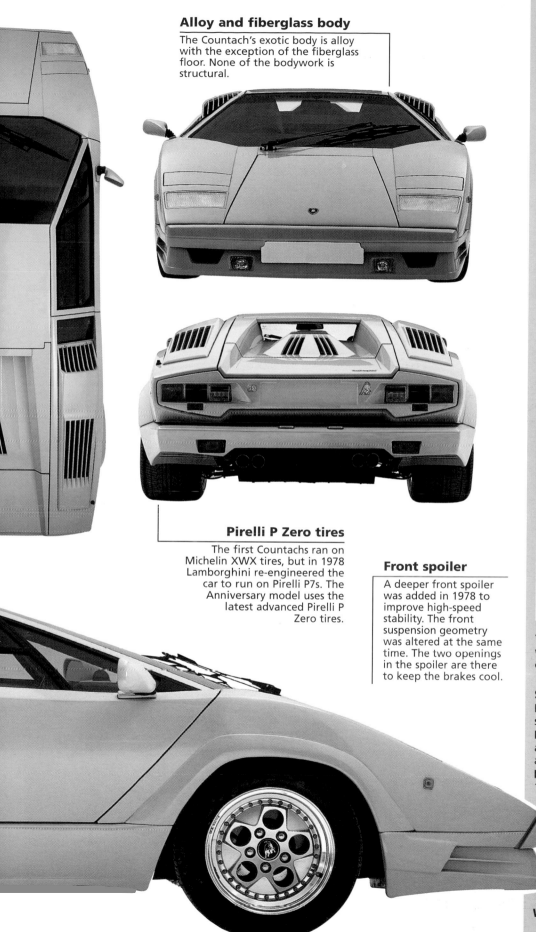

Alloy and fiberglass body
The Countach's exotic body is alloy with the exception of the fiberglass floor. None of the bodywork is structural.

Pirelli P Zero tires
The first Countachs ran on Michelin XWX tires, but in 1978 Lamborghini re-engineered the car to run on Pirelli P7s. The Anniversary model uses the latest advanced Pirelli P Zero tires.

Front spoiler
A deeper front spoiler was added in 1978 to improve high-speed stability. The front suspension geometry was altered at the same time. The two openings in the spoiler are there to keep the brakes cool.

Specifications
1990 Lamborghini Countach QV Anniversary

ENGINE
Type: V12
Construction: Alloy block and heads
Valve gear: Four valves per cylinder operated by four chain-driven overhead cams
Bore and stroke: 3.38 in. x 2.95 in.
Displacement: 5,167 cc
Compression ratio: 9.5:1
Induction system: Six Weber 44 DCNF downdraft carburetors
Maximum power: 455 bhp at 7,000 rpm
Maximum torque: 369 lb-ft at 5,200 rpm

TRANSMISSION
Five-speed manual

BODY/CHASSIS
Tubular steel spaceframe chassis with alloy and fiberglass two-door, two-seat body

SPECIAL FEATURES

NACA-style ducts were first used in aircraft and were very efficient at channeling air in at high speed.

You could drive the Countach flat out without the optional rear wing, usually chosen only for dramatic effect.

RUNNING GEAR
Steering: Rack-and-pinion
Front suspension: Double wishbones, coil springs, telescopic shocks and anti-roll bar
Rear suspension: Wishbones, trailing arms, double coil springs/shocks per side, and anti-roll bar
Brakes: Vented discs 11.8 in. dia. (front), 11 in. dia. (rear)
Wheels: Split-rim alloys, 8.5 in. x 15 in. (front), 12 in. x 15 in. (rear)
Tires: Pirelli P Zero, 225/50 VR15 (front), 345/35 VR15 (rear)

DIMENSIONS
Length: 162.9 in. **Width:** 78.7 in.
Height: 42.1 in. **Wheelbase:** 96.5 in.
Track: 58.7 in. (front), 63.2 in. (rear)
Weight: 3,188 lbs.

Lamborghini **DIABLO**

In the 1980s, Lamborghini was faced with a big problem: what could possibly replace the legendary but dated Countach? The answer was a car that was just as outrageous and even faster—the incredible Diablo.

"...the Raging Devil."

"You hear it down the Autostrada long before you see it. And as it passes at nearly 200 mph, there is only stunned silence. Now you're behind the wheel in command of nearly 500 horses and it's a little intimidating at first. But the all-wheel drive viscous differential puts this indecent amount of power to the road and the razor-sharp steering rewards your skill. Sixty mph rushes up in just over four seconds as the V12 sings the song of the Raging Devil."

Diablo's driving position is excellent and makes it easier to concentrate on driving this high-powered supercar to its limits.

Milestones

1985 Lamborghini president Emile Novaro asks his team to design a new car to replace the Countach. A 'super Countach' is created to evaluate parts for the forthcoming Diablo.

1990 The Diablo makes its debut at the beginning of the year.

After 17 years, the Countach was more than ready for a replacement.

1991 A four-wheel drive version, the Diablo VT appears. VT stands for Viscous Traction and the car has a center viscous coupling which puts up to 27 percent of drive to the front wheels.

1994 Lamborghini offers the Diablo SE which is stripped-down and lightened to make it even quicker.

German tuner Willi Koenig dragged even more power out of the V12.

1996 Lamborghini, now owned by Indonesian company Megatech, further increases the Diablo's appeal by launching the Diablo Roadster.

UNDER THE SKIN

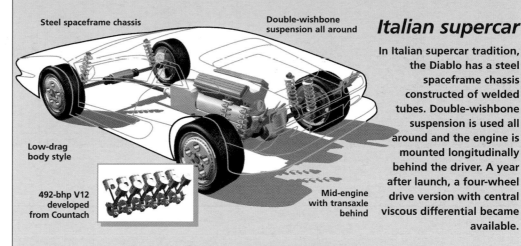

Steel spaceframe chassis

Double-wishbone suspension all around

Low-drag body style

492-bhp V12 developed from Countach

Mid-engine with transaxle behind

Italian supercar

In Italian supercar tradition, the Diablo has a steel spaceframe chassis constructed of welded tubes. Double-wishbone suspension is used all around and the engine is mounted longitudinally behind the driver. A year after launch, a four-wheel drive version with central viscous differential became available.

THE POWER PACK

Lamborghini's V12

The Diablo's 60-degree V12 is a distant descendant of Lamborghini's first V12 of 1963. By the early 1990s, the all-alloy V12 had grown from the Countach's 5 liters to 5.7 liters with a very short stroke crankshaft running in seven main bearings, allowing high rpm. Four chain-driven overhead cams operate 48 valves and each bank of cylinders has its own electronic engine management system controlling the ignition and fuel injection systems.

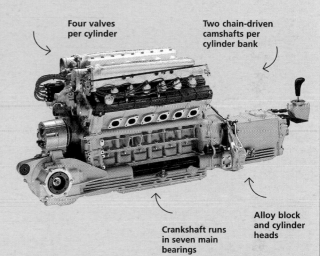

Four valves per cylinder

Two chain-driven camshafts per cylinder bank

Crankshaft runs in seven main bearings

Alloy block and cylinder heads

Rapid roadster

The Diablo Roadster, on sale in 1997, added one more ingredient to the 4WD Diablo—supercar performance with an open roof. The roof panel is made from carbon fiber, so it's easy for one person to lift off and stow over the engine cover.

Wind in your hair at over 180 mph!

Lamborghini DIABLO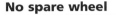

Twelve years since the Diablo was introduced, it's still a rare and thrilling sight. One look at Marcello Gandini's masterpiece tells you it really will go way beyond 190 mph.

No spare wheel

There's no room for even a space saver spare tire. Lamborghini's explanation? "Diablo drivers do not change wheels by the side of the road."

Twin rear radiators

Two radiators are needed to cool the big V12. Mounted at the rear of the engine bay, each is assisted by a large electric fan.

Forward-hinged doors

Like the Countach before it, the Diablo has long doors with single hinges that lift up and forward, each supported on a single gas strut.

Side-mounted oil coolers

The vents on the lower side panels feed air to the two oil coolers which are mounted directly ahead of the rear wheels.

Larger rear wheels

The Diablo needs massive tires to feed its power to the road and the 1991 model was equipped with large very low-profile Pirelli P Zero 335/35 ZR17s on 13 inch x 17 inch split rim alloy wheels.

Poor rear vision

Like most mid-engined supercars, the Diablo has extremely limited rear vision through the small rear window.

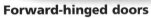

Alloy, composite and steel body

The Diablo's bodyshell is made from a mixture of materials. The roof is steel for strength, but the fenders and doors are alloy and a new composite material was used for the nose, engine cover, rockers and bumpers.

World's widest supercar

At 80.3 inches, the Diablo is wider than even Ferrari's bulky Testarossa, making it the widest supercar in the world.

Engine cooling vents

Once air has passed through the engine's twin radiators it exits through these large vents at the rear of the car.

Ventilation scoops

Cabin ventilation is provided via two small scoops in front of the windshield but, unlike the Countach, the Diablo is air conditioned.

Specifications
1991 Lamborghini Diablo

ENGINE

Type: Sixty-degree V12
Construction: Light alloy block and heads
Valve gear: Four valves per cylinder operated by four chain-driven overhead camshafts
Bore and stroke: 3.43 in. x 3.15 in.
Displacement: 5,729 cc
Compression ratio: 10.0:1
Maximum power: 492 bhp at 7,000 rpm
Maximum torque: 428 lb-ft at 5,200 rpm

TRANSMISSION

Five-speed manual

BODY/CHASSIS

Steel square-tube spaceframe chassis with two-door, two-seat coupe body in alloy, steel and carbon fiber

SPECIAL FEATURES

The vertically opening doors are a clever way of creating as much impact as gullwing doors, but without the same extremely difficult sealing problems.

RUNNING GEAR

Steering: Rack-and-pinion
Front suspension: Double wishbones with coil springs, telescopic shocks and anti-roll bar
Rear suspension: Double wishbones with twin coaxial spring shock units per side, and anti-roll bar
Brakes: Vented discs, 13 in. dia. (front), 11.2 in. dia. (rear)
Wheels: Multi-piece alloy, 8.5 in. x 17 in. (front), 13 in. x 17 in. (rear)
Tires: Pirelli P Zero 245/40 ZR17 (front), 335/35 ZR17 (rear)

DIMENSIONS

Length: 175.6 in.   **Width:** 80.3 in.
Height: 43.5 in.   **Wheelbase:** 104.3 in.
Track: 60.6 in. (front), 64.6 in. (rear)
Weight: 3,475 lbs.

Lamborghini MIURA

With one stroke, Ferruccio Lamborghini made Enzo Ferrari look foolish and his cars appear obsolete. Lamborghini beat Ferrari to the punch, building the world's first mid-engined supercar and the first with a quad-cam V12 engine.

"...sensation of the decade."

"The sensation of the 1966 Geneva Motor Show was also the sensation of the decade. Now this superb Bertone design is before you, and as you slide low into this gorgeous automobile, you realize why this is still one of the most desired cars ever built. Everything about this car is over-the-top: the colors, the sci-fi body design, the power and even the zero body roll that tempts you to push it until it suddenly breaks away."

There can be few more inviting cockpits than the Lamborghini Miura's. It's a car that truly begs to be driven hard.

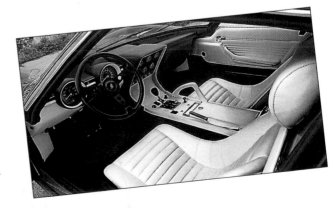

Milestones

1966 Lamborghini stuns the Geneva Motor Show by unveiling the 400 GT's replacement. The Miura is styled for Bertone by a rising star in the design world, Marcello Gandini.

The beautiful Touring-bodied 400 GT was Lamborghini's second model.

1967 Miura P400 production gets under way and 475 are built before the car is updated.

1969 The Miura S is introduced with the engine tuned to produce 370 bhp and torque increases to 286 lb-ft.

1971 The S turns into the SV with even more power, 385 bhp and an improved transmission, which makes the power easier to use.

1973 The world oil crisis helps bring about the end of Miura production.

Rear slats helped the style, but did little for rear visibility.

UNDER THE SKIN

Modern monocoque

While other Italian supercar builders were still using old-fashioned spaceframes, the Miura has a modern steel monocoque structure with the strength coming from massive sills and a large center tunnel, all three joined by large bulkheads. The engine is held in a folded steel frame behind the center bulkhead.

Front-mounted radiator

Mid-mounted engine

Double-wishbone rear suspension

Transverse V12

THE POWER PACK

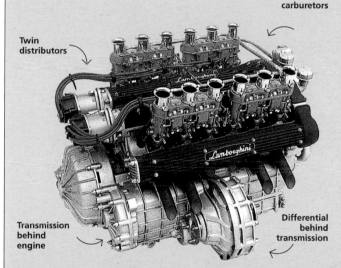

Twin distributors

Four Weber carburetors

Transmission behind engine

Differential behind transmission

Racing V12

The Miura's V12 was designed by the man who led development on the legendary Ferrari 250 GTO. For the very first Lamborghini (the 350 GT), Giotto Bizzarrini designed a quad-cam V12, with alloy block and heads, twin distributors and classical hemispherical combustion chambers. Even though there are only two valves per cylinder, it was originally more like a race than a road engine. It was slightly altered and refined before being installed in the Miura with an integral transmission.

The Miura SV

Last and best of the Miura line is the SV, introduced in 1971. It has more power (385 bhp), enough to take the top speed to over 174 mph and drops the 0-60 mph time to 6.8 seconds. A wider track under larger wheel arches improves the Miura's handling.

The SV was the last and best of the Miuras.

Lamborghini **MIURA**

Only three years after Lamborghini started making cars, the company produced the most exotic supercar the world had ever seen. It was as advanced as it was stunning, with its 4-liter V12 engine mounted behind the driver.

Alloy and steel bodywork

The main body section of the Miura is fabricated from steel for strength. Some panels, such as the engine cover and front section of the bodywork, are alloy to save weight.

Transverse V12

To make the Miura as compact as possible the engine is mounted transversely, making it the first transverse V12 supercar.

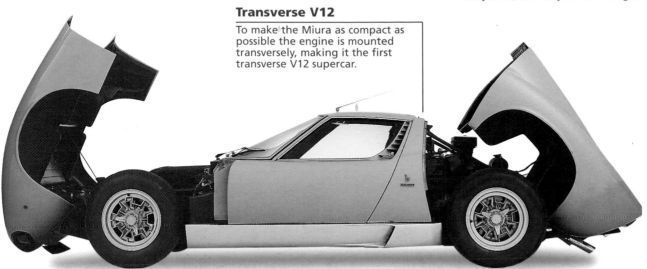

Transmission behind engine

With a transverse engine, there is no space for the transmission to be mounted in the usual place. The Miura's transmission is behind the engine, with the transmission and engine sharing the same oil.

Slatted engine cover

The great heat generated by a large V12 running fast in a small engine bay was vented through the open slatted engine cover, which did little to improve the view through the rear-view mirror.

Door frame air vents

One of the main styling features is the air vents—for the engine compartment—which are actually built into the door frame.

Tip forward lights

When not in use, the headlights fold back to follow the line of the bodywork, a styling feature used years later by Porsche on the 928.

Top-mounted anti-roll bar

The Miura follows racing car practice in many ways. For example, its rear anti-roll bar runs from the bottom wishbones up over the chassis.

Front-mounted radiator

Although the engine is mid-mounted, the radiator stays in the conventional place at the front where it is easier to cool with the help of two electric fans. It is angled to fit under the Miura's low sloping nose.

Specifications
1970 Lamborghini P400S

ENGINE
Type: V12
Construction: Light alloy block and heads
Valve gear: Two valves per cylinder operated by four chain-driven overhead camshafts
Bore and stroke: 3.23 in. x 2.44 in.
Displacement: 3,929 cc
Compression ratio: 10.7:1
Induction system: Four Weber downdraft carburetors
Maximum power: 370 bhp at 7,700 rpm
Maximum torque: 286 lb-ft at 5,500 rpm

TRANSMISSION
Five-speed manual

BODY/CHASSIS
Steel monocoque platform with steel and alloy two-door, two-seat coupe body

SPECIAL FEATURES

Stylized vents behind the doors provide air to the mid-mounted engine. Door handle is cleverly shaped to blend in with the styling.

The sloping headlights have distinctive 'eyebrows'; purely a styling feature.

RUNNING GEAR
Steering: Rack-and-pinion
Front suspension: Double wishbones with coil springs, telescopic shocks and anti-roll bar
Rear suspension: Double wishbones, with coil springs, telescopic shocks and anti-roll bar
Brakes: Solid discs, 11.8 in. dia. (front),12.1 in. dia. (rear)
Wheels: Magnesium 7 in. x 15 in.
Tires: Pirelli Cinturato GT70 VR15

DIMENSIONS
Length: 171.6 in.   **Width:** 71 in.
Height: 42 in.   **Wheelbase:** 98.4 in.
Track: 55.6 in. (front and rear)
Weight: 2,850 lbs.

Lancia STRATOS

The world's first purpose-built rally car was a huge success. The mid-engine Stratos won Lancia the World Rally Championship in 1974, 1975 and 1976.

"...tricky at the limit."

"You need considerable skill to drive a Stratos really fast. The gearshift is stiff, the steering light and the car twitchy thanks to the combination of its mid-engined layout and short wheelbase. Lift off suddenly through a corner and the car will snap into oversteer, which needs quick reactions to catch. If the suspension is not adjusted precisely, or the tire pressure exactly right, the car is even trickier at the limit. Although 190 bhp doesn't sound like much, in a light car it feels extremely quick."

Tight conditions and seriously off-set controls lead to an unusual driving style.

Milestones

1970 Coachbuilder
Bertone exhibits its Stratos concept car at the Turin Show in November.

1971 Bertone's next
Turin show car is the Stratos HF, inspired by the first car but one inch taller and designed to use a Ferrari V6 engine.

1973 Lancia
commissions Bertone to build the 500 cars required for race/rally homologation. The first Stratos win comes in the 1973 Spanish Firestone Rally and another car is second in the Targa Florio road race.

The Lancia Stratos won three Manufacturers' World Championships in 1974-76.

1974 Homologation
is completed and the Stratos wins the first of its three World Rally Championships.

1975/6 Stratos wins
more World Championships but production ceases in 1975.

The Stratos is a dramatic road car and a rally 'homologation special.'

UNDER THE SKIN

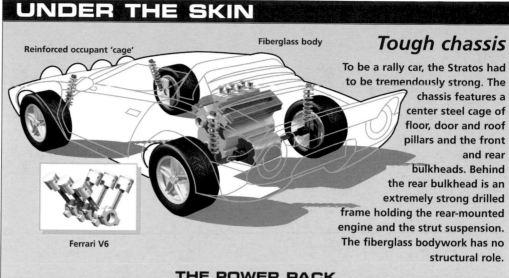

Reinforced occupant 'cage'   Fiberglass body

Ferrari V6

Tough chassis

To be a rally car, the Stratos had to be tremendously strong. The chassis features a center steel cage of floor, door and roof pillars and the front and rear bulkheads. Behind the rear bulkhead is an extremely strong drilled frame holding the rear-mounted engine and the strut suspension. The fiberglass bodywork has no structural role.

THE POWER PACK

Power potential

The Stratos' engine is a real thoroughbred—the V6 used in the Fiat and Ferrari Dinos, in its later iron-block Fiat form. It has four chain-driven overhead camshafts but only two valves per cylinder. For competition use, it could be tuned way beyond its standard 190 bhp, to as much as 580 bhp in one turbo-racing version. Rally versions also sometimes used four-valve cylinder heads where allowed. In standard form, it breathes through three downdraft twin-choke Weber carburetors.

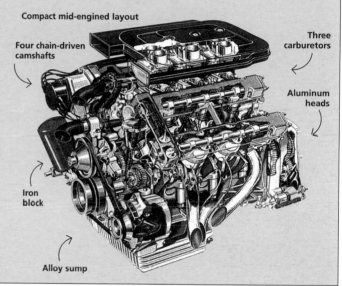

Compact mid-engined layout

Four chain-driven camshafts

Three carburetors

Aluminum heads

Iron block

Alloy sump

Competitive

There was little to match the Stratos and it won every major rally except the RAC and Safari, with 82 international wins in all, 16 in World Championship events. It was still surprisingly competitive in 1979 when Bernard Darniche won the Monte Carlo. It also won the Targa Florio in 1974.

The Stratos scored more than 80 international rally wins.

Lancia STRATOS

The Stratos looks almost as strange as the show car that gave it its name, yet it is extremely versatile. Not only was it a World Championship Rally-winning car, but also a successful road racer and a desirable roadgoing sports car.

Fiberglass body

None of the Stratos' body panels are load bearing, so they are made of fiberglass, keeping its weight to a minimum.

Ferrari Dino engine

By the time the Stratos was developed, Lancia had access to Ferrari engines and used its V6 'Dino' quad-cam V6 engine.

Wishbone front suspension

Classic twin-wishbone suspension is used in the front. The front wheel arches are bulged at the top to allow long wheel travel required in rallying.

Removable bodywork

Quick and easy mechanical access is vital in a rally car, so the front and rear sections of the Stratos lifts clear for maintenance. Both panels can also be completely removed quickly.

Short wheelbase

Mid-engined cars like the Stratos are normally very nimble and maneuverable, but the Stratos is more agile than most due to its short wheelbase.

Central spoiler

The tiny central spoiler is enough to provide extra downforce, supplementing the rear wing which helps keep the back of the car firmly on the road.

Vented disc brakes

Very effective brakes were required, so the Stratos has vented four-wheel discs, for improved stops.

Front-mounted radiator

The rear-mounted engine is cooled by a radiator in the front, with two electric fans, accounting for its louvered hood.

Specifications

1974 Lancia Stratos

ENGINE

Type: V6, quad cam

Construction: Cast-iron block and alloy cylinder heads

Valve gear: Two valves per cylinder operated by four chain-driven overhead camshafts

Bore and stroke: 3.64 in. x 2.36 in.

Displacement: 2,418 cc

Compression ratio: 9.0:1

Induction system: Triple Weber carburetors

Maximum power: 190 bhp at 7,000 rpm

Maximum torque: 166 lb-ft at 5,500 rpm

TRANSMISSION

Five-speed manual

BODY/CHASSIS

Fiberglass two-door, two-seat coupe body with folded sheet-steel frame

SPECIAL FEATURES

The wrap-around roof spoiler provides additional downforce and also helps guide air into the engine bay.

Rear bodywork lifts up as one panel.

RUNNING GEAR

Steering: Rack-and-pinion

Front suspension: Twin wishbones with coil springs, telescopic shocks and anti-roll bar

Rear suspension: MacPherson struts and anti-roll bar

Brakes: Vented discs, 9.9 in. dia. (front and rear)

Wheels: Alloy, 14-in. dia.

Tires: 205/70 VR14

DIMENSIONS

Length: 146 in. **Width:** 68.9 in.

Height: 68.9 in. **Wheelbase:** 85.5 in.

Track: 56.3 in. (front), 57.5 in. (rear)

Weight: 2,161 lbs.

 **UK** 1998

Light Car Company ROCKET

Conceived and engineered by top Formula 1 designer Gordon Murray, the Rocket may well be the ultimate driver's car. Nothing is as single-minded as this rapid, fun-packed machine.

"...dependent on the throttle."

"Getting into the Rocket feels like stepping into a Formula 1 racing car. Once situated in the supportive bucket seat, you have a full view of the road ahead. Fire up the engine and you instantly feel its high-revving idle behind you. Once you're on the road, truly sizzling performance takes over. Revving the engine up to its 11,000-rpm redline requires bravery. The handling is perfectly balanced, and dependent on the throttle."

Inside, the Rocket is similar to a Formula 1 race car, but it can accommodate two.

Milestones

1988 Gordon Murray

designs the fabulous McLaren MP4/4 Formula 1 racer, which enables the team to win all but one race, plus the drivers' and constructors' championships.

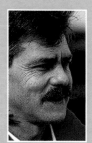

Gordon Murray designed the championship-winning Brabham BT 49 in addition to many other race cars.

1991 Joining forces

with Chris Craft to form the Light Car Company, Murray uses his Formula 1 experience and talent to produce the Rocket. The car is launched to an incredible public reception.

Another Murray-designed road car is the tremendous McLaren F1.

1995 Now under new sponsorship,

a factory is built especially to produce the Rocket. The price tag has risen to $70,500, which is low when the acceleration, handling and braking are taken into consideration, but high for such an impractical two seater.

UNDER THE SKIN

Like a racer

In concept, the Rocket aims to have the lightest possible weight and to deliver the greatest performance from its 1.0-liter engine. The multi-tubular spaceframe chassis is visible from inside the car. A second transmission and differential unit (which are in addition to the standard Yamaha transmission) support the rear suspension. The bodywork is composed of a simple fiberglass sandwich, and uses drilled four-wheel disc brakes.

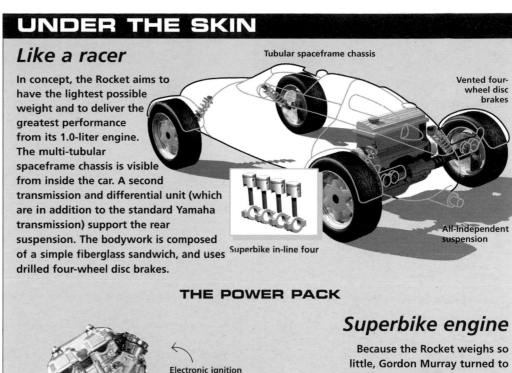

Tubular spaceframe chassis

Vented four-wheel disc brakes

All-independent suspension

Superbike in-line four

THE POWER PACK

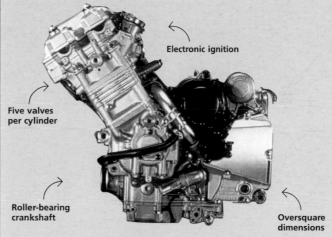

Electronic ignition

Five valves per cylinder

Roller-bearing crankshaft

Oversquare dimensions

Superbike engine

Because the Rocket weighs so little, Gordon Murray turned to the Yamaha FZR1000 superbike for its motive power. This powerful all-alloy, twin-cam, four-cylinder engine is massively oversquare. Each cylinder has five valves, and a roller-bearing crankshaft is used to deal with the engine's high rpm speeds. It has four Mikuni carbs, digital ignition and a high 12:1 compression ratio. The engine makes a respectable 143 bhp.

Exclusive

Launched in 1991, the Rocket has attracted much interest, particularly from the automotive press and enthusiasts. However, since production, only a small number have been built and the Rocket remains a very exclusive automobile. An owners club has been formed, originally chaired by the late former Beatle George Harrison.

With light weight, Rockets are an ideal basis for competition racers.

Light Car Company ROCKET

There is no car like the Rocket. Its engineering is superb, the quality impeccable, and the sensory delight complete. This machine lives up to its name in no uncertain terms.

Engine as stressed member

There is no chassis as such behind the cockpit. Instead—in true Formula 1 style—the transverse, mid-mounted Yamaha FZR1000 engine and secondary transmission act as stressed members and carry the rear suspension load.

Room for two

There is a second seat in the cockpit, behind the driver. It is accessed by removing a fairing situated behind the driver's head.

Ultra-powerful brakes

Considering its light weight, the Rocket's brakes are not large. They are, however, state-of-the-art cross-drilled discs and are self-venting with Brembo four-piston calipers. With that sort of braking power, there is no need for anti-lock technology.

Two transmissions

The Rocket uses a five-speed sequential transmission from the Yamaha FZR1000 superbike. There is even a second lever in the cockpit which changes the ratios in the rear differential for more relaxed cruising and also for reverse.

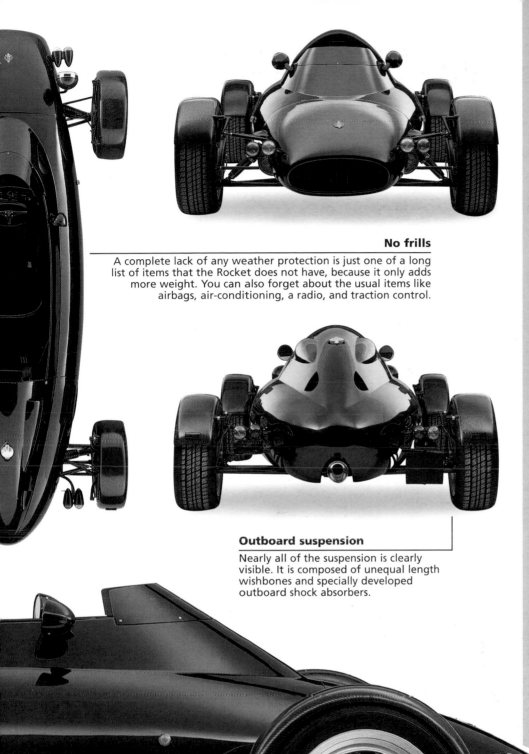

No frills

A complete lack of any weather protection is just one of a long list of items that the Rocket does not have, because it only adds more weight. You can also forget about the usual items like airbags, air-conditioning, a radio, and traction control.

Outboard suspension

Nearly all of the suspension is clearly visible. It is composed of unequal length wishbones and specially developed outboard shock absorbers.

Specifications

1998 Light Car Company Rocket

ENGINE
Type: In-line four
Construction: Aluminum block and head
Valve gear: Five valves per cylinder operated by double overhead camshafts
Bore and stroke: 3.0 in. x 2.2 in.
Displacement: 1,002 cc
Compression ratio: 12:1
Induction system: Four Mikuni carburetors
Maximum power: 143 bhp at 10,500 rpm
Maximum torque: 77 lb-ft at 8,500 rpm

TRANSMISSION
Five-speed sequential manual with twin-speed axle

BODY/CHASSIS
Tubular steel spaceframe chassis with fiberglass body

SPECIAL FEATURES

The twin rear differentials are a unique feature.

Special shock absorbers were designed for the Rocket by Showa.

RUNNING GEAR
Steering: Rack-and-pinion
Front suspension: Unequal length wishbones with coil springs and telescopic shock absorbers
Rear suspension: Unequal length wishbones with coil springs and telescopic shock absorbers
Brakes: Vented discs (front), solid discs (rear)
Wheels: Alloy, 15-in. dia.
Tires: 195/50 VR15

DIMENSIONS
Length: 143.5 in.   **Width:** 62.2 in.
Height: 37.5 in.   **Wheelbase:** 94.5 in.
Track: 62.0 in. (front), 62.5 in. (rear)
Weight: 882 lbs.

Lotus ELISE

Without the inspiration of founding genius Colin Chapman, few thought that Lotus could ever again build one of the world's very best sports cars, such as the original Elan. The Elise proved them wrong.

"...sets new standards."

"This Lotus sets new standards for small sports cars. Nothing comes close to the Elise's combination of a superbly comfortable ride coupled with absolutely precise handling in a car that's never thrown off-line by bumps and ridges and never bothered by the most demanding roads. The steering is incredibly light at parking speeds but still stays full of feel at really high speeds. That ability is combined with excellent acceleration off the line as 30 mph from a rest comes up in just 1.8 seconds."

Elise's interior is stark in the extreme. It's a car designed to excite the driver, not pamper him.

Milestones

1993 Lotus' chief engineer for vehicle design circulates a suggestion that the company build a lightweight sports car with the emphasis on handling and performance—in essence a modern version of the Lotus Seven. Later in the year, Rover becomes interested in the project, but when Rover is taken over by BMW in 1994, the idea goes no further.

Elise is the spiritual successor to the classic Lotus Seven.

1994 Management gives the go ahead for the Elise to become a production car. It is named after Romano Artioli's granddaughter.

1995 Elise makes its debut as one of the stars of the Frankfurt Motor Show.

The previous small Lotus was the Isuzu-engined, front-wheel drive Elan.

1996 Lotus Elise goes on sale in Europe with the company struggling to keep up with demand.

UNDER THE SKIN

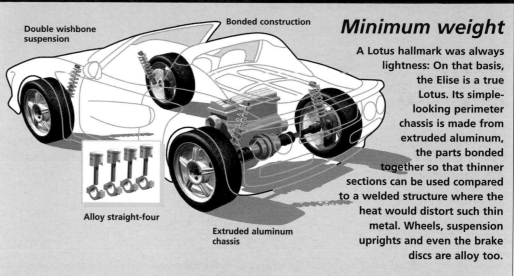

Double wishbone suspension

Bonded construction

Alloy straight-four

Extruded aluminum chassis

Minimum weight

A Lotus hallmark was always lightness: On that basis, the Elise is a true Lotus. Its simple-looking perimeter chassis is made from extruded aluminum, the parts bonded together so that thinner sections can be used compared to a welded structure where the heat would distort such thin metal. Wheels, suspension uprights and even the brake discs are alloy too.

THE POWER PACK

Rover power

The Elise uses Rover's modern and innovative K-series all-alloy, 16-valve, twin-cam engine. This has a novel form of sandwich construction with long bolts running the whole depth of the engine to hold it together. It's also a wet-liner design with the tiniest of water jackets to keep the engine compact. At 122 lb-ft its torque output is even more impressive than its outright power. Because the car is lightweight, it easily out-accelerates the similarly-engined MGF 1.8i, and even the more powerful MGF VVC.

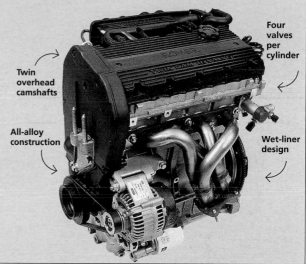

Twin overhead camshafts

All-alloy construction

Four valves per cylinder

Wet-liner design

Super-light

There are other all-alloy sports cars around such as the Renault Spider. Although the Renault only weighs 2,051 lbs., that's still 457 lbs. more than the tiny Elise: That's what helps make the Lotus Elise the best small sports car in the world.

Low overall weight has always been a Lotus trademark.

Lotus ELISE

Lotus knows that if you make a car as tiny and as light as possible, even a 1.8-liter engine will give it staggering performance, and naturally the Elise has the handling to match.

Front air vent

In an echo of the old Ford GT40 racers, the Elise has a deep vent in the hood through which the air that passes through the front-mounted radiator is extracted.

Twin-cam engine

The Rover K-series twin-cam engine which Lotus uses is the world's lightest 1.8-liter twin cam. That was one of the reasons why Lotus selected it.

Alloy chassis

The Elise is the first production car in the world to be made from alloy extrusions bonded together. The alloy sections are produced by Denmark's Hydro Aluminum Company.

Alloy suspension parts

Although the wishbones themselves are steel, the suspension uprights and brake discs are made of alloy, as are the brake, clutch and throttle pedals.

Stripped interior

To keep the Elise light, and to show off its state-of-the-art chassis construction, the interior trim is kept to a minimum.

Composite bodywork

As usual with Lotus, the Elise's body is made of fiberglass, but unlike other Lotus cars such as the Esprit (where it adds greatly to the car's strength), the Elise's chassis is so strong the body doesn't need to play a structural role.

Rear diffuser

For the driver who feels he needs more downforce, Lotus offers an optional rear diffuser to suck the car down to the road more securely.

Offset rear shocks

In a wishbone suspension, the spring/shock unit is usually in the center, but Lotus has mounted the shock ahead of the axle line.

Specifications
1996 Lotus Elise

ENGINE
Type: Rover K-series in-line four
Construction: Alloy block and cylinder head
Valve gear: Four valves per cylinder operated by two belt-driven overhead camshafts
Bore and stroke: 3.15 in. x 3.5 in.
Displacement: 1,796 cc
Compression ratio: 10.5:1
Induction system: MEMS electronic fuel injection
Maximum power: 118 bhp at 5,500 rpm
Maximum torque: 122 lb-ft at 3,000 rpm

TRANSMISSION
Five-speed manual

BODY/CHASSIS
Extruded bonded aluminum-alloy chassis with composite two-seat convertible body

SPECIAL FEATURES

Elise's high-tech chassis is built by bonding together the extruded aluminum components.

Large hood vents are necessary to flow cool air over the radiator.

RUNNING GEAR
Steering: Rack-and-pinion
Front suspension: Double wishbones with coil springs, telescopic shocks and anti-roll bar
Rear suspension: Double wishbones with coil springs and telescopic shocks
Brakes: Alloy/silicon carbide vented discs, 11.1 in. dia.
  Wheels: Alloy, 5.5 in. x 15 in. (front), 7 in. x 16 in. (rear)
  Tires: 185/55 VR15 (front), 205/50 VR16 (rear)

DIMENSIONS
Length: 146.7 in. **Width:** 71.7 in.
Wheelbase: 90.6 in.   **Height:** 47.3 in.
  Track: 56.7 in. (front), 57.2 in. (rear)
Weight: 1,594 lbs.

Lotus ESPRIT V8

In 1996, the Lotus Esprit finally got the engine its wonderful chassis deserved. Squeezing a twin-turbo V8 into the Esprit transformed it into a serious Ferrari-fighting supercar.

"...world class steering."

"The 349-bhp Esprit V8 shows why Lotus takes lessons from no one when it comes to making a car perform and handle. Its steering sets it apart—one of the world's best power-assisted systems tells you exactly what's going on, giving you the confidence to place the car with absolute precision. Staggering acceleration and outright performance make up for its few faults. The transmission is awkward and the twin-turbo still lacks the immediate throttle response of the best normally-aspirated engines."

Leather-trimmed cabin is far higher quality than in early Esprits. Placement of the controls and driving position are not ideal, though.

Milestones

1976 The first Esprit appears, with a 160-bhp version of the Lotus 2-liter twin-cam four.

1980 After minor changes in 1978 to produce the S2, Lotus enlarges the engine to 2.2 liters. The Turbo Esprit is launched, with 210 bhp, stronger chassis, revised suspension, wider wheels and tires.

Early Esprits had much sharper lines, but the overall shape is similar to the current car.

1987 Body is radically restyled in-house with rounded, softer lines. Turbo now has 215 bhp.

1989 SE (Special Equipment) Turbo model is the best yet, with handling improvements and power up to 264 bhp.

1993 Further improvement produces the S4 (0-60 mph in 5.0 seconds) and the lightweight Sport 300.

1995 S4S combined the best of S4 and Sport 300 with 285 bhp, dropping 0-60 mph to under five seconds.

1996 Esprit V8 is launched with a new 349-bhp twin-turbo V8 engine.

UNDER THE SKIN

Typically Lotus

The fiberglass bodywork covers an absolutely typical Lotus chassis, with a deep center backbone fabricated from sheet steel and featuring double wishbones at the front and a multi-link layout at the rear. The chassis had to be changed surprisingly little to take the V8 and the suspension is slightly upgraded to take the extra 110 lbs. of the new engine.

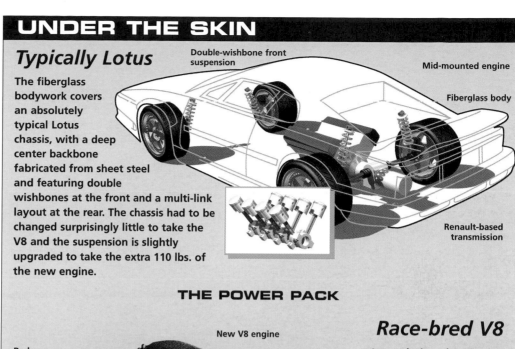

Double-wishbone front suspension

Mid-mounted engine

Fiberglass body

Renault-based transmission

THE POWER PACK

New V8 engine

Red cam covers—like a Ferrari

Four camshafts

Two small Garrett T25 turbochargers

Race-bred V8

Lotus designed an engine capable of 520 bhp for GT1-class racing and detuned it for the street-legal Esprit, so it's more than strong enough to cope with 349 bhp. It's all alloy and extremely compact, with four cams, 32 valves and hydraulic lifters, and it uses two small Garrett T25 turbochargers to overcome turbo lag. While outright power is impressive its torque output (295 lb-ft at 4,250 rpm) and the spread of torque from 2,250 rpm up is even more so.

GT racer

In 1996, a V8 Esprit took on the likes of the McLaren F1 and the new Porsche 911 GT1 in international GT racing and proved that the basic design was extremely competitive. A lack of funds and development slowed the car, but its career was short because Lotus intended to use its V8 in the racing Elise.

Flames spurt from the Lotus's twin turbos at Le Mans in 1996.

Lotus ESPRIT V8 🇬🇧

You have to look closely to tell the difference between the Esprit S4 and the new V8 because Lotus spent all the money it could afford on doubling the car's number of cylinders and turbochargers.

Twin intercoolers

To lower the temperature of the intake air (making it denser and helping combustion and power) each turbocharger has an intercooler.

Split-rim wheels

The V8 Esprit comes equipped with OZ Racing split-rim alloys which are different sizes front and rear, the fronts being 'only' 8.5-inches wide.

New V8 engine

This is the first production Lotus V8, a 349-bhp all-alloy quad-cam design. A more powerful version powers Lotus's new racing Elise at events like the 24 Hours of Le Mans.

Upgraded ABS

One significant change between four-cylinder and V8 Esprits is the switch to Kelsey-Hayes four-channel ABS, which gives some of the most impressive braking in the world.

Kevlar reinforcement

Kevlar is used to reinforce the roof pillars to improve roll-over protection and increase their strength without making them thicker. Kevlar is also used in the sills to help make the whole structure stiffer.

Renault transmission

Lotus first used Renault parts in the Europa in the 1960s and turned to Renault once again in the Esprit. The V8 uses a transmission derived from that used in the fast GTA and A610 Renault Alpine sports cars.

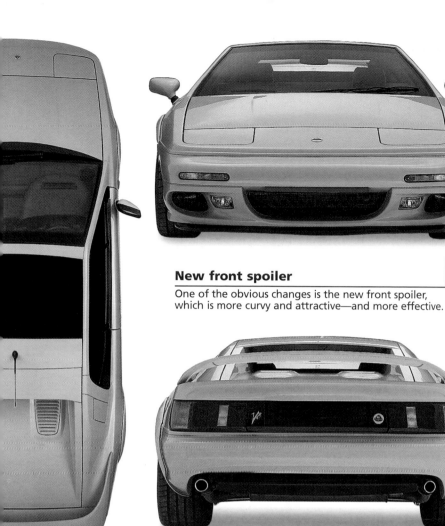

New front spoiler

One of the obvious changes is the new front spoiler, which is more curvy and attractive—and more effective.

Huge tires

The V8's tires are much larger than those used on the first Esprit over 20 years ago, particularly at the back of the car where they are 285/35 ZR18s running on wheel rims 10 inches wide.

Front radiator

Because there's no room in the engine bay for a radiator, it's mounted at the front where it cools more effectively.

ENGINE

Type: V8
Construction: Alloy block and heads
Valve gear: Four valves per cylinder operated by four overhead camshafts and hydraulic lifters
Bore and stroke: 3.19 in. x 3.27 in.
Displacement: 3,506 cc
Compression ratio: 8.0:1
Induction system: Electronic fuel injection with twin Garrett T25 turbochargers
Maximum power: 349 bhp at 6,500 rpm
Maximum torque: 295 lb-ft at 4,250 rpm

TRANSMISSION

Five-speed manual

BODY/CHASSIS

Sheet steel fabricated backbone chassis with fiberglass two-door coupe body

SPECIAL FEATURES

V8 uses two turbochargers, one for each bank of cylinders, to give the engine better throttle response than if it used a larger single turbo.

One of the easiest ways to tell the V8 apart is by its new front spoiler with its larger air intakes.

RUNNING GEAR

Steering: Rack-and-pinion
Front suspension: Double wishbones with coil springs, telescopic shocks and anti-roll bars
Rear suspension: Upper and lower links, coil springs, telescopic shocks and anti-roll bar
Brakes: Vented discs, 11.7 in. dia. (front), 11.8 in. dia. (rear); ABS
Wheels: OZ Racing split-rim alloys, 8.5 in. x 17 in. (front), 10 in. x 18 in. (rear)
Tires: 235/40 ZR17 (front), 285/35 ZR18 (rear)

DIMENSIONS

Length: 173.9 in.   **Width:** 78 in.
Height: 45.3 in.   **Wheelbase:** 95.3 in.
Track: 59.8 in. (front and rear)
Weight: 2,968 lbs.

Maserati GHIBLI

The modern Ghibli takes its name from the great Maserati supercar of the 1970s. But in place of the big V8 is a small 2.8-liter twin-turbo— it's one of the Italian company's most powerful small engines.

"...a car for the brave."

"A short wheelbase and a staggering amount of power and torque suggest that the Ghibli is a car for the brave, and to a certain extent this is true. When the small V6 gets beyond 3,000 rpm, the twin turbos force air into the engine, which is matched by the correct amount of fuel, rocketing the car to 100 mph in just 13.6 seconds. The interior oozes Italian style. However, the car feels dated on the road because it lacks the body contour of rivals like the BMW M3."

In contrast to many contemporary cars, the Ghibli's dash is quite angular.

Milestones

1989 Maserati returns to the high-performance world with the Shamal, a development of the Biturbo. Aggressively flared fenders and wide wheels distinguish it from the Biturbo.

The Ghibli can trace its lineage back to the Biturbo of the 1980s.

1992 At the Turin Motor Show, the

Shamal's styling is toned down for the new Ghibli. The main difference is the use of a small 2.0-liter twin-turbo V6 to generate 305 bhp and a top speed of 160 mph.

The new 3200 GT was added to the Maserati range in 1998.

1995 A GT version of the Ghibli appears.

It has a 2.8-liter V6 and an automatic transmission.

1997 Named after the successful Ghibli Open Cup racing series, the street-legal 330-bhp Ghibli Cup appears.

UNDER THE SKIN

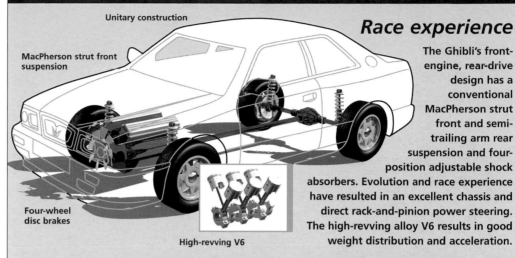

Unitary construction

MacPherson strut front suspension

Four-wheel disc brakes

High-revving V6

Race experience

The Ghibli's front-engine, rear-drive design has a conventional MacPherson strut front and semi-trailing arm rear suspension and four-position adjustable shock absorbers. Evolution and race experience have resulted in an excellent chassis and direct rack-and-pinion power steering. The high-revving alloy V6 results in good weight distribution and acceleration.

THE POWER PACK

Torquey V6

Years of twin-turbo Maserati experience result in an incredible engine: an all-alloy short-stroke 2.8-liter V6 which likes to run at a very high rpm. It has the expected four overhead camshafts opening four valves per cylinder, precise distributorless electronic ignition and multipoint fuel injection resulting in 280 bhp. The biggest surprise, however, is the torque output, which at 317 lb-ft is greater than that of many larger engines.

Electronic fuel injection

Four valves per cylinder

Aluminum-alloy block and cylinder heads

Forged-steel crankshaft

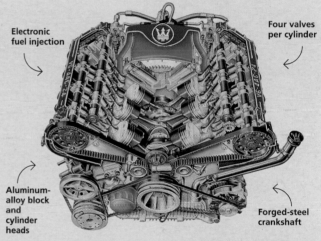

Homologation

In addition to the Ghibli GT, there is also the Ghibli Cup—a limited edition, roadgoing version of the Cup series Ghibli racers. It is powered by a 2.0-liter version of the V6, which kicks out an amazing 330 bhp. It comes with a standard six-speed Getrag manual transmission, upgraded suspension, wider wheels and Brembo brakes.

The Ghibli Cup looks similar to the GT but is more powerful.

Maserati GHIBLI

Although the Biturbo is not considered a true Maserati by many, it did spawn a whole new generation of Maseratis, including the excellent Shamal and its successor, the exceedingly fast Ghibli.

Torque monster V6

Although not quite as powerful as the Maserati Cup, the Ghibli GT's 2.8-liter V6 is much more torquey, making it better suited to normal driving conditions.

Four-piston calipers

The Ghibli has some of the best brakes of any production car, thanks to the use of four-piston Brembo calipers operating huge vented discs at the front and solid discs at the rear. ABS is standard.

Five-speed transmission

Since 1994, the GT has been offered with either manual or automatic transmissions. This particular example has a German Getrag five-speed, whereas the later Ghibli Cup model uses a six-speed.

Stiffened suspension

The MacPherson strut front and semi-trailing arm rear suspension is lowered and the spring rates stiffened to further improve handling.

Decade old design

Outwardly, the Ghibli looks modern, but its styling and inner structure date back to the 1981 vintage Biturbo. Unlike its ancestor, however, the Ghibli handles better.

Quad tailpipes

A dual exhaust set up culminates in twin tailpipes each with dual tips. The Cup model has a different exhaust with twin outlets.

1994 Maserati Ghibli GT

ENGINE

Type: V6

Construction: Light-alloy block and heads

Valve gear: Four valves per cylinder operated by twin overhead camshafts per bank of cylinders

Bore and stroke: 3.70 in. x 3.42 in.

Displacement: 2,790 cc

Compression ratio: 7.6:1

Induction system: Electronic fuel injection with twin IHI turbochargers and intercoolers

Maximum power: 280 bhp at 5,500 rpm

Maximum torque: 317 lb-ft at 3,750 rpm

TRANSMISSION

Getrag five-speed manual

BODY/CHASSIS

Steel monocoque with two-door coupe body

SPECIAL FEATURES

The GT's dual exhaust pipes exit through the rear valance.

The distinctive Maserati Trident symbol is carried on the plenum cover.

RUNNING GEAR

Steering: Rack-and-pinion

Front suspension: MacPherson struts with adjustable shock absorbers and anti-roll bar

Rear suspension: Semi-trailing arms with coil springs, adjustable shock absorbers and anti-roll bar

Brakes: Vented discs, 12-in. dia. (front), solid discs, 12.4-in. dia. (rear)

Wheels: Alloy split rim, 8 x 17 in. (front), 9 x 17 in. (rear)

Tires: 215/45 ZR17 (front), 245/40 ZR17 (rear)

DIMENSIONS

Length: 166. 2 in. **Width:** 69.9 in.

Height: 51.2 in. **Wheelbase:** 99.0 in.

Track: 59.6 in. (front), 59.4 in. (rear)

Weight: 2,998 lbs.

Mazda **MIATA**

The sports car effectively died in the 1980s, but in 1989 Mazda single-handedly brought it back to life with the Miata. Compact, pretty and with sharp handling, it was a real sales success.

"...Sporty, fun and economical."

"Sitting behind the leather-trimmed wheel of the MX-5 Miata, you could almost be in one of the great British sports cars of the 1960s. Everything is simply laid out, with no superfluous decoration, and the gear shifter is just inches from the steering wheel. Through corners, the car is finely controllable and while it may not be particularly fast in a straight line, the Miata is sporty, fun and economical in every sense of the words."

Like many Japanese cars, the Miata's interior is simplistic yet very functional.

Milestones

1989 Mazda launches
the MX-5 Miata at the Detroit Motor Show in January, exclusively for the American market initially.

There is no doubt that the Miata's styling owes a great deal to the original Lotus Elan.

1990 The MX-5 is launched
in Europe. In Japan, the model is sold as the Eunos Roadster.

1993 To cope with increasing
weight, Mazda installs a 1.8-liter engine. A much cheaper base model, with a less-powerful 90-bhp, 1.6-liter engine, is also still available.

The sporty Miata had its own popular race series.

1997 Production ends
as a new MX-5 Miata is launched at the Tokyo Motor Show. More than 450,000 of the original version have been produced, making it one of the best-selling sports cars ever.

UNDER THE SKIN

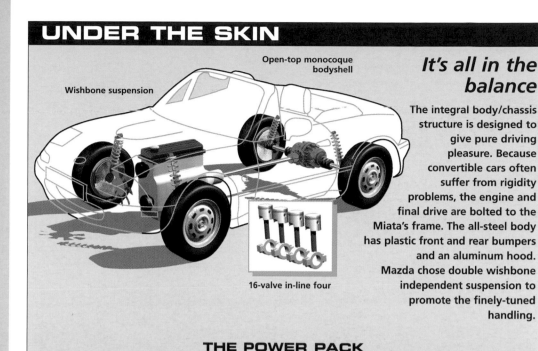

Wishbone suspension

Open-top monocoque bodyshell

16-valve in-line four

It's all in the balance

The integral body/chassis structure is designed to give pure driving pleasure. Because convertible cars often suffer from rigidity problems, the engine and final drive are bolted to the Miata's frame. The all-steel body has plastic front and rear bumpers and an aluminum hood. Mazda chose double wishbone independent suspension to promote the finely-tuned handling.

THE POWER PACK

Efficient and reliable

Mazda derived its 1.6-liter B6-ZE four-cylinder twin-camshaft engine from the 323 range, but fine-tuned it to increase its redline by 200 rpm. With a catalytic converter, its output was a modest, but perfectly adequate, 116 bhp. In 1993, to counter the Miata's growing weight, Mazda introduced a 1.8-liter fuel-injected engine, which produced 131 bhp. The latest 1998 model Miata has a higher power output of 140 bhp and 119 lb-ft of torque.

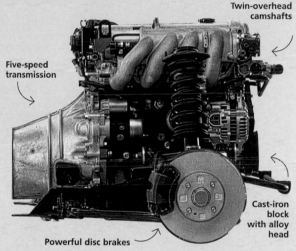

Twin-overhead camshafts

Five-speed transmission

Cast-iron block with alloy head

Powerful disc brakes

Face-lifted fun

Although some may miss the novelty of the pop-up headlights, the new 1998 Mazda Miata is a great improvement over its predecessor. Increased power, a stiffer bodyshell, more modern styling, and even sharper handling make it a sure winner.

After nine years, a facelift was much deserved for the Miata.

Mazda MIATA

Recognized around the world as the car that brought back sports car fun, the Miata is brilliant in its simplicity. It is the all-purpose, popular sports car champion.

Classic body styling

Many people compare the Miata with the late, great Lotus Elan. Its shape and proportions are very similar and the general feel is also remarkably consistent with the sports car classics of the 1960s.

Simple top

Anyone used to fiddling with old convertibles will find the new Mazda's top quite simple. You don't even have to unbuckle your seat belt—just press two buttons, fold back the two levers and push the top back.

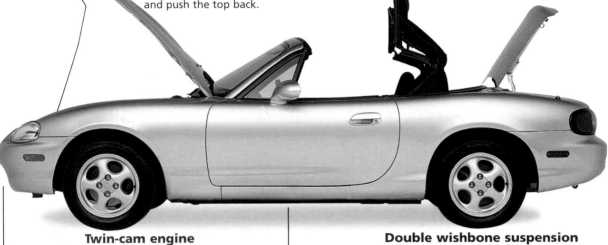

Twin-cam engine

With an aluminum twin-cam cylinder head and cast-iron block, the four-cylinder engine was state of the art rather than cutting edge. A three-way catalytic converter keeps emissions to a minimum.

Double wishbone suspension

Few cars that are not used on the race track or come from a Ferrari showroom have independent suspension all around with unequal-length double wishbones. This helps to give the Miata extremely capable handling.

Rack-and-pinion steering

The high-geared, power-assisted rack-and-pinion steering is incredibly fast-reacting. It means you can almost 'feel' your way around bends by simply flexing your wrists.

Powerplant sub-frame

Mazda put the engine, transmission and final drive in a separate subframe. This increases rigidity and isolates the major moving parts to make driving more refined.

Specifications

1998 Mazda Miata 1.8

ENGINE

Type: In-line four

Construction: Cast-iron block and aluminum alloy head

Valve gear: Four valves per cylinder operated by twin overhead camshafts

Bore and stroke: 3.26 in. x 3.34 in.

Displacement: 1,839 cc

Compression ratio: 9.0:1

Induction system: Multi-point electronic fuel injection

Maximum power: 140 bhp at 6,500 rpm

Maximum torque: 119 lb-ft at 5,500 rpm

TRANSMISSION

Five-speed manual or four-speed automatic

BODY/CHASSIS

Steel monocoque with separate engine/transmission subframe and two-door roadster body with some aluminum and plastic panels

SPECIAL FEATURES

The new 1.8-liter engine has more horsepower than the previous unit.

For a more modern look, the new Miata no longer has pop-up lights.

RUNNING GEAR

Steering: Power-assisted rack-and-pinion

Front suspension: Unequal length double wishbones with coil springs, shocks and anti-roll bar

Rear suspension: Unequal length double wishbones with shocks and anti-roll bar

Brakes: Vented discs front, discs rear

Wheels: Cast-alloy, 14-in. dia.

Tires: 185/60 HR14

DIMENSIONS

Length: 155.3 in.   **Width:** 66 in.

Height: 47.3 in.   **Wheelbase:** 89.2 in.

Track: 55.9 in. (front), 57 in. (rear)

Curb weight: 2,108 lbs.

Mazda RX-7

After its 1991 Le Mans win, Mazda unveiled the third-generation RX-7. Lighter and faster than ever, its twin turbochargers gave 255 bhp and a top speed of over 155 mph. The RX-7 had gone from a sports car to a junior league supercar in one leap.

"...the RX-7 has it all."

"Power, performance, handling; the RX-7 has it all. There's no turbo lag and the engine runs quickly to 4,000 rpm: With both turbos spinning furiously, it really takes off as it soars to its 6,500 rpm power peak. The steering is razor sharp and the RX-7 responds instantly to every driver input. You can place the Mazda exactly where you want it, and then adjust its cornering line with the throttle. There's only one (acceptable) penalty—the rock hard ride."

Stark, black plastic interior is typically Japanese, but the RX-7 is more about performance and driver enjoyment than luxury.

Milestones

1967 Mazda introduces the Cosmo, its first real sports car, pioneering a twin-rotor Wankel engine.

1978 With experience gained from the Cosmo, Mazda designs the first RX-7, again with a twin-rotor engine but with a simple live rear axle.

Racing experience helped in the development of the road car.

1985 The second-generation RX-7 appears, still with a rotary engine of course, but now bigger, with hints of Porsche styling and a more advanced independent rear suspension.

1991 Mazda finally wins the 24 Hours of Le Mans outright after years of participation with rotary cars. Later this year, the third-generation RX-7 appears. It is in a different class from the previous car and one of the best handling sports cars ever made.

1996 With Mazda looking at a smaller version of their frontline rotary sports car, the RX-01 show car, the days of the twin-turbo RX-7 are numbered and the decision is made to end production.

UNDER THE SKIN

Lightweight

The RX-7 was designed to be light and as fast as possible. The shell is steel but all the advanced double-wishbone suspension components are alloy, daringly bolted directly to the body without rubber bushes to help give more precise handling. For the same reason, alloy cross braces are featured to help make the body as stiff as possible and a frame joins the transmission to the final drive.

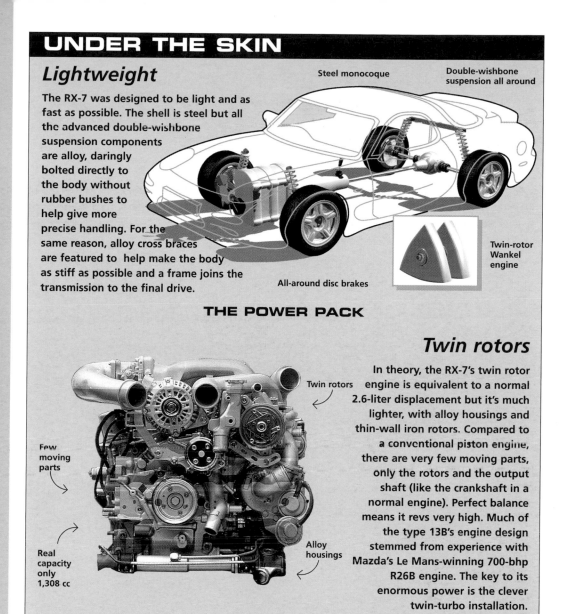

Steel monocoque

Double-wishbone suspension all around

All-around disc brakes

Twin-rotor Wankel engine

THE POWER PACK

Twin rotors

In theory, the RX-7's twin rotor engine is equivalent to a normal 2.6-liter displacement but it's much lighter, with alloy housings and thin-wall iron rotors. Compared to a conventional piston engine, there are very few moving parts, only the rotors and the output shaft (like the crankshaft in a normal engine). Perfect balance means it revs very high. Much of the type 13B's engine design stemmed from experience with Mazda's Le Mans-winning 700-bhp R26B engine. The key to its enormous power is the clever twin-turbo installation.

Twin rotors

Few moving parts

Real capacity only 1,308 cc

Alloy housings

Curvaceous

With the RX-7, Mazda cleverly combined the best of oriental and western styling. The Japanese influence comes in the number and form of scoops and vents which are functional and add interest to the shape. Western influence shows in the simple but elegant lines.

The third generation RX-7 has the power to match its stunning looks.

Mazda

The RX-7 shows just how much progress Mazda has made since 1978, when the RX-7 had less than half the power of the 1997 model. Even the second-generation car was nearly 100-bhp less powerful.

Comprehensive equipment

Although the RX-7 was designed to be as light as possible, it went on sale in some markets with a long list of standard equipment, such as leather seats, cruise control and air conditioning—all of which made the car heavier.

Twin-rotor engine

There are no conventional reciprocating valves in a twin-rotor Wankel engine. The turbos force the fuel mixture through ports uncovered in the rotor housing as the rotors sweep around.

Rear wing

Mazda installed a rear wing to increase high-speed stability at the expense of aerodynamic drag, thus reducing the car's top speed.

Pop-up lights

Mazda had no choice but to use pop-up lights—the car was so low it was the only way to get the headlamps up to the required legal height.

Limited slip differential

To avoid power-wasting wheelspin in corners, a limited slip differential was installed. The efficient worm-drive Torsen (standing for 'torque sensing') type was used.

'Powerplant frame'

A light but strong cast-alloy beam is used to connect the transmission and the final drive. It eliminates movement in the drivetrain and makes the car's structure stiffer.

Vented discs

The RX-7's high performance was matched by its braking. Four-wheel 11.6 inch dia., vented discs are used with standard anti-lock braking.

Oil cooler ducts

Oil coolers supplement the normal radiator. Air is ducted to the coolers via vents on either side of the radiator opening.

Equal size tires

It's not unusual for cars with this much power to have larger rear tires, but they are all 225/50 ZR16s on the RX-7.

Specifications
1993 Mazda RX-7

ENGINE
Type: Twin-rotor Wankel
Construction: Alloy housing with cast-iron rotors and end plates
Valve gear: Circumferential porting
Bore and stroke: N/A
Displacement: 1,308 cc (nominal)
Compression ratio: 9.0:1
Induction system: Bosch electronic fuel injection with twin Hitachi HT 12 turbochargers
Maximum power: 255 bhp at 6,500 rpm
Maximum torque: 217 lb-ft at 5,000 rpm

TRANSMISSION
Five-speed manual transmission

BODY/CHASSIS
Unitary construction steel two-door coupe body with supplementary light-alloy 'powerplant frame'

SPECIAL FEATURES

An alloy beam connecting the transmission and final drive stiffens the car's structure, improving handling and reducing snatch in the drivetrain. With a short, curved roof, the RX-7's sunroof cannot slide back inside the headlining.

RUNNING GEAR
Steering: Rack-and-pinion
Front and rear suspension: Double unequal-length wishbones, coil springs, telescopic shocks and anti-roll bar
Brakes: Four-wheel vented discs, 11.6 in. dia. with anti-lock system
Wheels: Cast-alloy 8 in. x 16 in.
Tires: Bridgestone Expedia 225/50 ZR16

DIMENSIONS
Length: 168.5 in. **Width:** 68.9 in.
Height: 48.4 in. **Wheelbase:** 95.5 in.
Track: 57.5 in. (front and rear)
Weight: 2,800 lbs.

McLaren F1

When the seven-time Formula One world champions at McLaren decided to build their first road car, they created the world's most exotic and most expensive supercar, the 627-bhp F1.

"...nothing even comes close."

"The F1's central seating layout allows the driver perfect visibility over the small, neat instrument pod and a comfortable driving position without the compromises of lesser supercars. The F1 is not a difficult car to drive. It is as civilized as it is fast and with over 600 bhp there's none faster—it accelerates faster than a Formula 1 car. Steering response is instant, but like a race car, it needs expert hands to really get it to perform to its limits."

The driver's seat is in the center of the car, with passenger's seats set slightly back, to improve driver vision and comfort.

Milestones

1992 The McLaren F1 appears on May 28 at the Monaco GP. Production starts the following year.

1995 McLaren produces the GTR version for international GT racing. Power is increased to 636 bhp with different cam profiles and remapped engine management. The GTR wins its first race and goes on to win Le Mans.

McLaren's F1 is one of the

easiest supercars to drive.

1996 In celebration of the Le Mans win, McLaren introduces the LM version with 668 bhp and an extra 41 lb-ft of torque. Changes are made to the floor shape (for aerodynamics), bumpers, rear suspension and steering. 0-60 mph time falls to 3.2 seconds.

F1's striking lines were penned by designer Peter Stevens.

1997 McLaren brings out the new GTR racer, heavily revised and much lighter with a smaller, 600-bhp 6-liter engine and improved aerodynamics.

UNDER THE SKIN

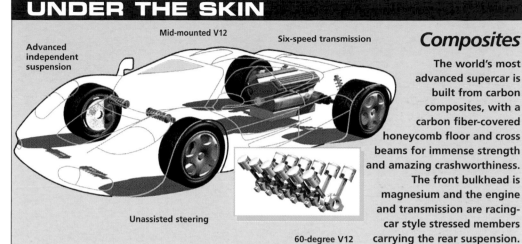

Advanced independent suspension · Mid-mounted V12 · Six-speed transmission · Unassisted steering · 60-degree V12

THE POWER PACK

Composites

The world's most advanced supercar is built from carbon composites, with a carbon fiber-covered honeycomb floor and cross beams for immense strength and amazing crashworthiness. The front bulkhead is magnesium and the engine and transmission are racing-car style stressed members carrying the rear suspension.

BMW M-Power

Built for McLaren by BMW Motorsport in Munich, the 6-liter quad-cam, alloy V12 has continuously variable intake valve timing to produce the greatest power and torque at all engine speeds. Each cylinder has its own individual ignition coil. It's compact and thanks to many magnesium-alloy parts and even a carbon composite intake air box, it's also extremely light (573 lbs.). It uses four chain-driven overhead camshafts operating four valves per cylinder. Four catalytic convertors ensure emissions are clean.

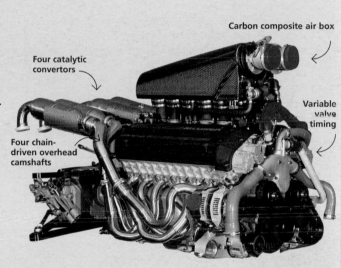

Four catalytic convertors · Carbon composite air box · Four chain-driven overhead camshafts · Variable valve timing

Le Mans winner

The most expensive F1, the LM version, was built to celebrate McLaren's win at Le Mans in 1995. Based on the F1 GTR, it produces 668 bhp, is 132 lbs. lighter and has a claimed top speed of 225 mph. It's slower than the standard car due to drag from the large spoiler.

1997's GTR was significantly revised, especially from an aerodynamic standpoint.

McLaren **F1** 🇬🇧

McLaren managed to build the world's best supercar in its very first attempt with the Gordon Murray-designed F1. Unlike most other street-legal supercars, it was good enough to win Le Mans.

Luggage storage

Because space in the front luggage compartment is limited, there are other clever compartments, such as those ahead of the rear wheels, to increase total luggage space.

BMW V12 engine

McLaren commissioned the quad-cam V12 engine from BMW. Light, compact and powerful, its output rose from 550 bhp in 1994 to 668 bhp, all without turbochargers.

Plasma-coated glass

Plasma sprayed onto the inside of the outer glass laminate provides a tint and a heating element to defrost or defog the windshield extremely fast.

'Brake and balance' spoiler

Under heavy braking the spoiler rises at an angle of 30 degrees, generating rear downforce and overcoming the usual pitching.

Formula 1 brakes

The F1's huge vented brakes made by Brembo are as effective as Formula 1 brakes before they were made of carbon fiber.

Six-speed transmission

Six speeds allow the McLaren to have the first five ratios close together and a high 'overdrive' sixth for relaxed high-speed travel.

Survival cell

If the F1 crashes at very high speeds, the occupants are protected by a survival cell; an extremely strong cockpit made of carbon fiber.

Ground effects

Air passing through the venturi tunnels under the F1 drops in pressure, generating 'ground effect' and sucking the car firmly down on the road at high speeds.

Central driver's seat

The driver sits in the center to get the best view and control and also the best weight distribution. Passengers sit on either side, and slightly behind him.

Impact absorbing muffler

The muffler is huge, with a capacity of 65 liters and it has a dual purpose, also acting as a crumple zone in the case of a rear impact.

Specifications
1995 McLaren F1

ENGINE

Type: V12 quad cam by BMW
Construction: Alloy block and heads
Valve gear: Four valves per cylinder operated by four chain-driven overhead cams with variable intake timing
Bore and stroke: 3.39 in. x 3.43 in.
Displacement: 6,064 cc
Compression ratio: 10.5:1
Maximum power: 627 bhp at 7,300 rpm
Maximum torque: 479 lb-ft at 4,000 rpm

TRANSMISSION

Six-speed manual

BODY/CHASSIS

Carbon fiber two-door, three-seat coupe with carbon fiber and Nomex/alloy honeycomb monocoque chassis

SPECIAL FEATURES

The rear spoiler rises under heavy braking, increasing rear downforce and stopping the nose diving.

The driver sits in the center of the car, with a full racing harness rather than a normal seat belt.

RUNNING GEAR

Steering: Rack-and-pinion
Front suspension: Twin wishbones, coil springs, shocks and anti-roll bar
Rear suspension: Twin wishbones with coil springs and shocks
Brakes: Brembo discs, 13.1 in. dia. (front), 12 in. (rear)
Wheels: Magnesium 9 in. x 17 in. (front), 11.5 in. x 17 in. (rear)
Tires: 235/45 ZR17 (front) and 315/40 ZR17 (rear)

DIMENSIONS

Length: 169 in.   **Width:** 72 in.
Height: 45 in.   **Wheelbase:** 107 in.
Track: 62 in. (front), 58 in. (rear)
Weight: 2,245 lbs.

Mercedes-Benz 300SL

Created from Mercedes-Benz's first Le Mans-winning racing car, the 300SL 'Gullwing' was a race car built for the road. In the mid-1950s, it gave a few lucky drivers 1990s levels of performance.

"...spectacular and rare."

"Few have ever seen, let alone driven, one of the most coveted cars Mercedes Benz ever produced. Those lucky souls don't think about the astronomical price this 300SL would bring, they just enjoy this spectacular and rare automobile. It's actually fast enough to keep up with many modern sports cars. The transmission has synchros on all four gears and is easy to use, although the clutch is heavy. The ride is firm, like a sports cars should be, but definitely not old fashioned."

The cabin of the Gullwing was not a nice place to be on a hot day—it didn't have opening windows. Owners opened their doors in traffic for fresh air.

Milestones

1952 Mercedes builds its first postwar racer, the 300SL coupe. With a spaceframe chassis, Gullwing doors and 172 bhp from its six-cylinder engine, it leads its first event, the 1952 Mille Miglia, but finishes second before winning Le Mans and the Carrera Panamericana.

The 300SL: successful in racing.

1954 The street-legal version of the 300SL is introduced at the New York Motor Show.

1955 Production gets fully underway and the 300SL—with fuel injection replacing carburetors—is faster than the racer. It is also more than twice as expensive as a Chevrolet Corvette in the U.S.

1957 The Gullwing is discontinued after 1,400 have been built and the open Roadster appears at the Geneva Show. The chassis has been redesigned to allow conventional doors and the swing-axle rear suspension has been improved. Its top speed is up to 150 mph.

1961 Disc brakes with servo assistance are added to the car, vastly increasing stopping power. Production ends in 1963.

UNDER THE SKIN

Spaceframe

The 300SL has almost a full spaceframe chassis made from a network of small tubes. It is a lightweight yet strong design, but it means the chassis sides are too high for conventional doors, hence the lift-up Gullwing type. The swing-axle rear suspension makes for tricky handling at the limit as does the all-drum brake setup.

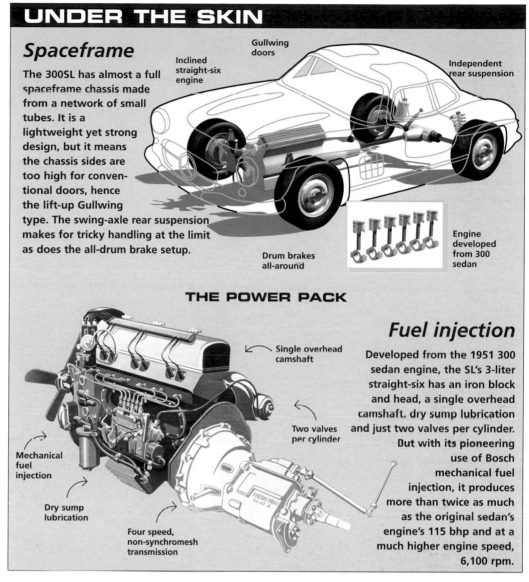

Inclined straight-six engine

Gullwing doors

Independent rear suspension

Engine developed from 300 sedan

Drum brakes all-around

THE POWER PACK

Single overhead camshaft

Two valves per cylinder

Mechanical fuel injection

Dry sump lubrication

Four speed, non-synchromesh transmission

Fuel injection

Developed from the 1951 300 sedan engine, the SL's 3-liter straight-six has an iron block and head, a single overhead camshaft, dry sump lubrication and just two valves per cylinder. But with its pioneering use of Bosch mechanical fuel injection, it produces more than twice as much as the original sedan's engine's 115 bhp and at a much higher engine speed, 6,100 rpm.

Open top fun

Although the Gullwing is more highly valued, the Roadster is by far the nicer car to drive. It had much more power, revised rear suspension for more predictable handling and a much less claustrophobic cabin than the cramped Gullwing.

Although not as desirable, the 300SL Roadster is an easier car to live with.

Mercedes-Benz 300SL

The dramatic looks of the world's first postwar supercar were dictated by the racing car chassis under the body which made the Gullwing doors essential.

Hood bulges

Only one bulge is required, to clear the injection system—the other is there to balance the design.

Tilting steering wheel

Getting in and out of the 300SL could be difficult because of the high sills, so the steering wheel tilts to make room.

Wheel arch 'eyebrows'

These were purely a styling feature (the early racing coupes didn't have them) intended to appeal to the American market where most 300SLs were sold.

Deep side sills

Deep sill panels are necessary to cover up the sides of the spaceframe chassis.

Finned brake drums

The 300SL is stopped by massive alloy brake drums which are finned to help cooling. They were still not very effective and were eventually replaced by discs on the Roadsters.

Air extractors

To get a good flow of air through the cabin, twin extractors are incorporated into the rear of the roof.

Alloy doors

To ease the strain on the roof-mounted hinges, the doors are made from alloy rather than steel. It also helps save weight overall, as do the alloy hood and trunk lid.

Flush fitting door handles

The door handles are almost too small to notice. The end is pushed in to reveal the whole handle. Handles like these inspired the designers of the Fiat Barchetta in the 1990s.

Sedan engine

Apart from its pioneering use of fuel injection, the specification of the 300SL's engine was quite ordinary due to its sedan origins.

Specifications
1955 Mercedes 300SL

ENGINE

Type: Straight-six
Construction: Cast-iron block and head
Valve gear: Two valves per cylinder operated by single overhead camshaft
Bore and stroke: 3.35 in. x 3.46 in.
Displacement: 2,996 cc
Compression ratio: 8.5:1
Induction system: Bosch mechanical fuel injection
Maximum power: 240 bhp at 6,100 rpm
Maximum torque: 216 lb-ft at 4,800 rpm

TRANSMISSION
Four-speed manual

BODY/CHASSIS
Steel and alloy two-door coupe with steel spaceframe chassis

SPECIAL FEATURES

Engines in early cars tended to overheat so these large vents were added to allow hot engine-bay air to escape.

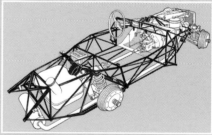

Spaceframe chassis was made light and strong, and was based on that of SL racers.

RUNNING GEAR
Steering: Recirculating ball
Front suspension: Twin wishbones with coil springs and telescopic shocks
Rear suspension: Swinging half axles with coil springs and telescopic shocks
Brakes: Drums all around
Wheels: Steel discs 5 in. x 15 in.
Tires: Crossply 6.7 in. x 15 in.

DIMENSIONS
Length: 178 in.   **Width:** 70 in.
Height: 49.7 in.   **Wheelbase:** 94 in.
Track: 54.5 in. (front), 56.5 in. (rear)
Weight: 2,850 lbs.

MGB

One of the best-loved sports cars the world has ever known, the MGB also still retains its status as one of the longest-lived. In Roadster form it quickly became the archetypal British sports car of the post-war era.

"...pure enjoyment."

"In 1962 the MGB was a fine expression of the ideal sports car, and one of the most affordable on the market. The steering is communicative and the handling predictable—at least until you hit a bump, when it gets knocked out of shape all too easily. The B-series engine is tractable from low revs but does not have a high redline. For pure enjoyment the MGB was hard to beat and it is a fine value today."

The MGB has a classic and simple interior, although the steering wheel seems huge for a sports car by today's standards.

Milestones

1962 After a four-year
development period, the MGB Roadster is first shown to the public at the Motor Show at Earl's Court in England.

1963 A fiberglass
hardtop becomes a popular and inexpensive option.

The six-cylinder MGC can be recognized by the big hood bulge.

1964 The engine
receives a five-bearing crankshaft and an oil cooler becomes standard.

1965 The Roadster
is joined by a GT coupe model.

The MGB was available in GT and Roadster forms. These are post-1974 'rubber bumper' models.

1967 A new Mk II
model receives an all-synchromesh transmission and the option of automatic transmission. The MGB remains in production until 1980.

UNDER THE SKIN

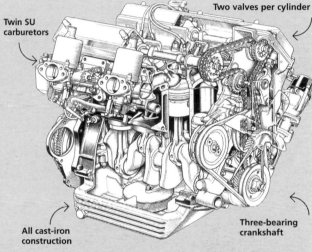

Coil-sprung front suspension

Live rear axle

Monocoque construction

Trusty B-series

Classically British

The MGB was designed by the company's Chief Engineer, Sydney Enever, following the principles of and using many components from his previous MGA. It therefore has the proven coil spring and wishbone front suspension and a live rear axle with semi-elliptic leaf springs. The MGB departs from previous MG practice in its use of unitary (monocoque) construction.

THE POWER PACK

Rugged engine

MG could have opted to fit the powerful 108-bhp, twin-cam engine which it had developed for the MGA in the MGB. However, the poor reliability record of this powerplant led to the choice of the well-proven overhead-valve B-series engine. For the MGB it is bored out to 1,796 cc, and power has increased from 86 bhp to 95 bhp. The bore castings are siamesed and the main bearings beefed up, but the head gear remains as before. One of its best characteristics is a flat torque curve.

Twin SU carburetors

Two valves per cylinder

All cast-iron construction

Three-bearing crankshaft

Prized original

In MG circles, an early example of the original Roadster with the three-bearing engine is highly desirable. Built for only two years, it is rare to find in good condition and is keenly sought after. The earliest car represents the purest expression of the MGB form.

The early MGB is a prized collector's car.

MGB 🇬🇧

There is no doubt that the MGB is what sports cars are supposed to be like. An open-topped, two-seater, front-engined, rear-wheel drive car is the way to travel.

Monocoque construction

Unlike all previous MG cars, the 'B' was designed around monocoque principles, using strong, double-skinned sills. This simplified the production process, reduced build costs and made the overall package more effective.

Leaf-sprung rear

Although MG experimented with an independently sprung rear end, the MGB has a live rear axle. It is suspended by semi-elliptic leaf springs and uses lever-arm shock absorbers.

Chrome bumpers

Early MGBs are colloquially known as 'chrome bumper' cars to distinguish them from the Federal-equipped 'rubber bumper' cars. Aesthetically, the original chrome finish is more pleasing and retains the familiar slatted grill of the older MGs.

Wind-up windows

Unlike all previous MG sports cars, which stuck with the old British custom of removable side windows or curtains, the MGB has glass windows that are opened and closed using a hand crank. Though this is a matter of course in U.S. built cars, it's considered a a luxury for MG owners.

Spacious cabin
By sports car standards, room inside the cockpit is very generous and the driver and passenger have no difficulty getting comfortable.

Specifications

1962 MGB Roadster

ENGINE
Type: In-line four-cylinder
Construction: Cast-iron block and head
Valve gear: Two valves per cylinder operated by a single camshaft via pushrods
Bore and stroke: 3.16 in. x 3.5 in.
Displacement: 1,796 cc
Compression ratio: 8.8:1
Induction system: Two SU carburetors
Maximum power: 95 bhp at 5,500 rpm
Maximum torque: 110 lb-ft at 3,500 rpm

TRANSMISSION
Four-speed manual (overdrive optional)

BODY/CHASSIS
Monocoque chassis with two-door steel open body

SPECIAL FEATURES

The early three-bearing MGB is recognizable by its 'pull' door handles.

The MGB was designed with chrome bumpers, but post-1974 cars have rubber bumpers to meet the U.S. safety regulations.

RUNNING GEAR
Steering: Rack-and-pinion
Front suspension: Wishbones with coil springs and lever-arm shock absorbers
Rear suspension: Live axle with semi-elliptic springs and lever-arm shock absorbers
Brakes: Discs (front), drums (rear)
Wheels: Steel, 14-in. dia.
Tires: 165/70 14

DIMENSIONS
Length: 153.2 in. **Width:** 59.9 in.
Height: 49.4 in. **Wheelbase:** 91 in.
Track: 49.2 in. (front), 49.2 in. (rear)
Weight: 2,080 lbs.

Panoz ROADSTER

Despite its youth, the Panoz has made big waves as a superfast, hand-built roadster. Its bare-boned style and advanced aluminum construction make it intriguing and exciting to drive.

"...pure, modern magic."

"To get into the Panoz you have to open a tiny door and step over the sill. The narrow cockpit feels like one of the great sports cars of the 1960s, but when you turn the key and hear the throb of a Mustang V8, you know this has to be a 1990s car. Floor the throttle and you are catapulted off the line at tremendous speed. The pleasure of prowling along twisty roads in the Roadster is pure, modern magic."

The cockpit may be in the spirit of 1960s sports cars, but ergonomically-designed seats and a heater are welcomed modern features.

Milestones

1994 Danny Panoz

sets out to create a car that offers pure driving thrills for the American driver. Having taken over an Irish motorsports company that had an inspired car design, Panoz develops the vehicle to meet U.S. regulations and shows the Roadster this year.

In 1997, Panoz entered the GT endurance series with the sleek new GTR-1.

1995 At the Geneva Motor Show, the Swiss

tuning company Rinspeed presents a mildly-modified version of the Panoz, known as the Rinspeed Roadster.

The latest car from Panoz is the sleek Esperante coupe.

1996 Panoz AIV

Roadster (AIV stands for aluminum-intensive vehicle) debuts in the U.S. to a rapturous reception from the press.

UNDER THE SKIN

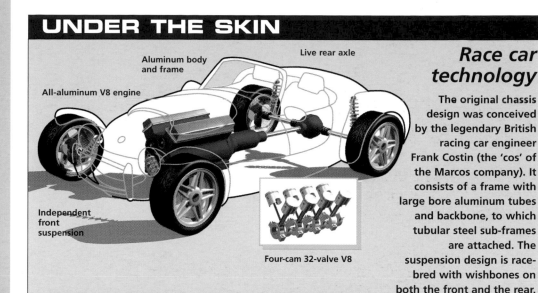

Aluminum body and frame
Live rear axle
All-aluminum V8 engine
Independent front suspension
Four-cam 32-valve V8

Race car technology

The original chassis design was conceived by the legendary British racing car engineer Frank Costin (the 'cos' of the Marcos company). It consists of a frame with large bore aluminum tubes and backbone, to which tubular steel sub-frames are attached. The suspension design is race-bred with wishbones on both the front and the rear.

THE POWER PACK

Mustang Cobra V8 power

Taken straight from the current Ford Mustang Cobra, the 4.6-liter modular V8 is state-of-the-art and features four camshafts, 32 valves, fuel injection and sophisticated emissions control. In both the Mustang Cobra and the Panoz Roadster this engine develops 305 bhp, and when combined with the aluminum construction of the Panoz it produces outstanding performance and refinement. The use of a standard Ford engine also means that the Panoz Roadster can be serviced by Ford dealerships.

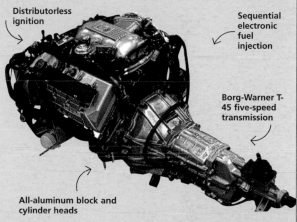

Distributorless ignition
Sequential electronic fuel injection
Borg-Warner T-45 five-speed transmission
All-aluminum block and cylinder heads

Hand-built

Although it also produces the Esperante Le Mans road-racing car, Panoz offers just one version of its hand-built AIV Roadster. However, there is a range of options to suit an individual's preferences. A sports suspension package is available, as are a trunk-mounted luggage rack and side wind deflectors.

Panoz owners can personalize their cars with factory options.

Panoz ROADSTER

With Ford Mustang Cobra V8 power, awesome performance and few creature comforts, the American-built Panoz AIV Roadster is the true Shelby Cobra of the 1990s.

Different suspension settings

Two different suspension settings are available: standard and sport. The latter offers stiffer spring rates and a much firmer, but still comfortable ride.

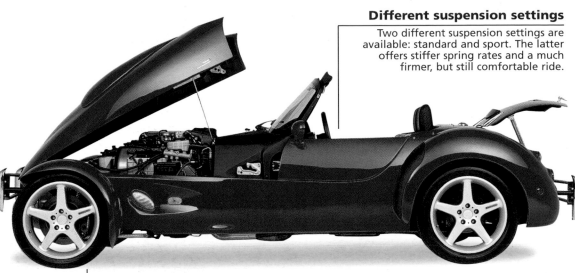

Ford sub-systems

Choosing standard Ford parts for the engine, drivetrain, and electrics results in excellent reliability and servicing that can be carried out by Ford dealerships.

Race car chassis

The chassis is descended from an original design by the ex-Marcos and Lotus engineer Frank Costin. The integrity of Costin's original aluminum frame is retained, despite modifications to house the drivetrain.

Ultra-low profile tires

The wide, 18-inch alloy wheels are fitted with ultra-low profile BF Goodrich Competition T/A tires—245/40 at the front and 295/35 at the rear.

Classically simple interior

Inside, in classic sports car fashion, form follows function. Interior choices are burr walnut or carbon fiber trim, and dark- or beige-colored leather upholstery. Air-conditioning and a monster stereo are available as options.

Elemental styling

The original style of the Panoz was co-created by Danny Panoz and Freeman Thomas, and draws on many influences, particularly the Jaguar E-type and Austin Healey, as well as traditional American hot rods.

Aircraft-technology body

The Roadster's aluminum body panels are built for safety and strength and are similar to those used on aircraft.

Vented disc brakes

The Roadster has one of the world's most effective braking systems, consisting of large diameter vented disc brakes on all four corners. The front discs also boast twin-piston calipers.

Specifications
1997 Panoz AIV Roadster

ENGINE

Type: V8
Construction: Aluminum cylinder block and heads
Valve gear: Four valves per cylinder operated by two chain-driven overhead camshafts per cylinder bank
Bore and stroke: 3.55 in. x 3.54 in.
Displacement: 4.6 liters
Compression ratio: 9.9:1
Induction system: Fuel injection
Maximum power: 305 bhp at 5,800 rpm
Maximum torque: 300 lb-ft at 4,800 rpm

TRANSMISSION

Borg-Warner T-4S five-speed manual

BODY/CHASSIS

Aluminum space frame with two-door roadster body

SPECIAL FEATURES

Small 'cycle-wing' fenders turn with the front wheels to prevent debris from being thrown over the car and driver.

Extensive use of aluminum results in a very light, but strong, frame.

RUNNING GEAR

Steering: Power rack-and-pinion
Front suspension: Unequal length wishbones, with coil spring/shock units, and anti-roll bar
Rear suspension: Unequal length wishbones with coil/spring shock units, and anti-roll bar
Brakes: Vented disc brakes all around
Wheels: Aluminum, 18-in. dia.
Tires: 245/40 ZR18 (front), 295/35 ZR18 (rear)

DIMENSIONS

Length: 155 in.   **Width:** 76.5 in.
Height: 47 in.   **Wheelbase:** 104.5 in.
Track: 65 in. (front), 64.2 in. (rear)
Weight: 2,459 lbs.

Porsche 356

Although Porsche had designed several vehicles for other manufacturers, the 356 was the first car to be built with a Porsche badge. It was Volkswagen Beetle-based and was an outstanding sports and racing car.

"...can be pushed hard."

"With its eager, smooth and free-revving engine, the 356 is a car that begs to be driven hard. Even in normal driving, the engine sees 5,000 rpm frequently. The flat-four is very flexible and will pull evenly, if not vigorously, from very low speeds in third and top gears. Lift-off oversteer on the later cars was quickly remedied, so even unskilled drivers can push the 356 on twisty roads with the power on to make the most of the traction."

With more embellishments than earlier examples, the 356B is still a real joy to drive.

Milestones

1947 Ferry Porsche starts work on the first Porsche-badged car—the 356.

1948 The prototype hits the road. It uses a mid-mounted VW engine.

The Porsche 356C was also available in a much sought-after convertible form.

1949 The Type 356 makes its motor show debut at Geneva in the spring.

The more sophisticated 911 followed in the 356's footsteps.

1951 A 356 wins its class at Le Mans.

1955 The updated 356A is introduced with Speedster and Carrera variants.

1959 The new 356B has a facelifted body and more powerful engines.

1963 The final 356C is launched. It is replaced by the 911 in 1965.

UNDER THE SKIN

Beetle-based

Like the Beetle, the 356 has a platform chassis, with a trailing arm and torsion bar front suspension and swing axles and torsion bars at the rear. Drum brakes front and rear are standard, although discs arrived on the 356C in 1963. This model also introduced ZF worm-and-peg steering.

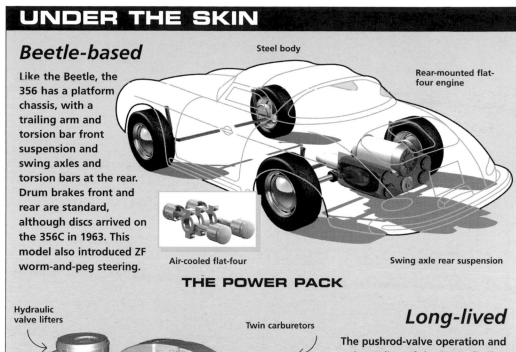

Steel body

Rear-mounted flat-four engine

Air-cooled flat-four

Swing axle rear suspension

THE POWER PACK

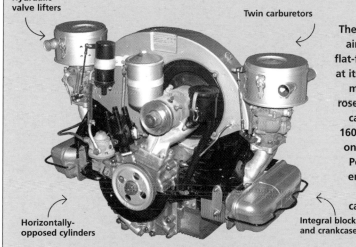

Hydraulic valve lifters

Twin carburetors

Horizontally-opposed cylinders

Integral block and crankcase

Long-lived

The pushrod-valve operation and air-cooling of the 356's all-alloy flat-four engine may hint strongly at its VW roots, but this is a much more sophisticated unit. Power rose from just 40 bhp in the early cars to 95 bhp in the final 356C 1600SC model, and the unit lived on in the entry-level 911-bodied Porsche—the 912. The ultimate engine, however, is the Carrera unit with twin overhead camshafts per cylinder bank. In 2.0-liter form it could take the 356 to 125 mph.

Speedster

Probably the most recognized of all Porsche 356 variants is the Speedster. First introduced in 1954, it was designed as a no-frills convertible. It was a slow seller, therefore not too many were built. This makes it highly desirable today.

During its four year production run, the Speedster hardly changed.

Porsche 356

From its introduction in 1948, the 356 was improved annually. It matured from a crude little tourer to a sophisticated and competitive sports car.

Karmann-built bodywork

This car has the rare Karmann Hardtop bodywork. Introduced for the 1961 model year, it was built for only one year. It is basically a cabriolet with a welded-on hard top.

Choice of engines

The air-cooled flat-four engine comes in 1,100-, 1,300-, 1,500- and 1,600-cc versions and produces between 40 and 95 bhp in pushrod form. The quad-cam Carrera unit is highly specialized and is developed from racing practice.

Beetle-derived suspension

Although derived from the Volkswagen Beetle, the swing axle rear suspension has few components in common, particularly on later cars. Springing is by torsion bars with telescopic shock absorbers.

Worm and peg

The worm-and-peg steering was a VW item, and was improved by a steering damper from the type A onward. On the 365C a ZF steering box was used.

Synchromesh transmission

Early cars have 'crash' non-synchromesh transmissions, but a full synchro transmission on later cars is noted for its precision and 'engineered' feel despite its lengthy linkage.

Drum brakes all around

Twin leading shoe hydraulic brakes are found on all 356s up until the C model of 1963, which features four-wheel discs.

Specifications

1961 Porsche 356B 1600S

ENGINE

Type: Flat-four

Construction: Alloy block and heads

Valve gear: Two valves per cylinder operated by a single camshaft via pushrods and rockers

Bore and stroke: 3.25 in. x 2.91 in.

Displacement: 1,582 cc

Compression ratio: 8.5:1

Induction system: Two Zenith carburetors

Maximum power: 75 bhp at 5,000 rpm

Maximum torque: 85 lb-ft at 3,700 rpm

TRANSMISSION

Four-speed manual

BODY/CHASSIS

Steel platform chassis with steel Karmann bodywork and welded-on hard top

SPECIAL FEATURES

These sport mirrors are most often seen on later 356B and C models.

By 1965, amber rear turn signals were fitted on European-specification cars.

RUNNING GEAR

Steering: Worm-and-peg

Front suspension: Torsion bars with trailing arms, telescopic shock absorbers and anti-roll bar

Rear suspension: Swing axles with torsion bars and telescopic shock absorbers

Brakes: Hydraulic drums (front and rear)

Wheels: Steel discs, 4.50 x 15 in.

Tires: Radials, 165 x 15

DIMENSIONS

Length: 155.5 in. **Width:** 65.7 in.

Height: 50.7 in. **Wheelbase:** 82.6 in.

Track: 51.5 in. (front and rear)

Weight: 2,059 lbs.

Porsche 911 SPEEDSTER

Who could forget the 356 Speedster of the 1950s, with its sleek low looks and cut-down windshield? Certainly not Porsche, which recreated, in both name and spirit, this great classic. This modern-day Speedster is based on the immortal 911.

"...ferocious flat-six engine."

"Any Porsche 911 is a unique driving experience, but the Speedster feels special. You sit low, held firmly in place by narrow, supportive seats. The windshield comes right up to your line of sight and when the roof is up you feel very confined. The ferocious flat-six engine rockets you down the road with tremendous velocity. The sport suspension and wide tires mean that the limit of adhesion is reached only at very high speeds."

The Speedster's sporty interior benefits from supportive seats and easy-to-read gauges.

Milestones

1987 Porsche displays a prototype 911 Speedster at the Frankfurt Motor Show. It has a contoured tonneau cover and single windshield for just the driver.

The Speedster shares the name with the 1955 356A convertible.

1989 The production 911 Speedster is launched as a limited-run special at the end of the then-current 911's production run. Production finishes by July, with 465 cars sold in Germany and 1,225 having been exported. The only fully open-top 911 still available is the cabriolet.

The current 911 is available in convertible form.

1998 Following the launch of the new water-cooled 911 coupe, a convertible model is introduced.

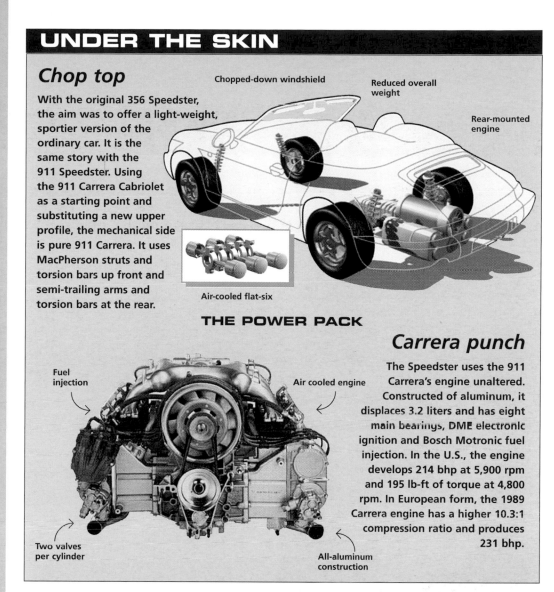

Chop top

With the original 356 Speedster, the aim was to offer a light-weight, sportier version of the ordinary car. It is the same story with the 911 Speedster. Using the 911 Carrera Cabriolet as a starting point and substituting a new upper profile, the mechanical side is pure 911 Carrera. It uses MacPherson struts and torsion bars up front and semi-trailing arms and torsion bars at the rear.

Chopped-down windshield

Reduced overall weight

Rear-mounted engine

Air-cooled flat-six

THE POWER PACK

Fuel injection

Air cooled engine

Two valves per cylinder

All-aluminum construction

Carrera punch

The Speedster uses the 911 Carrera's engine unaltered. Constructed of aluminum, it displaces 3.2 liters and has eight main bearings, DME electronic ignition and Bosch Motronic fuel injection. In the U.S., the engine develops 214 bhp at 5,900 rpm and 195 lb-ft of torque at 4,800 rpm. In European form, the 1989 Carrera engine has a higher 10.3:1 compression ratio and produces 231 bhp.

Unique style

The Speedster occupies a special place in 911 history. It may not be the fastest 911 variant, but it is utterly unique with its distinctive styling. It also has the benefit of being extremely rare and collectable and will always command a good price.

A chopped windshield gives the Speedster a sleek, low look.

Porsche SPEEDSTER

The Porsche 911 is one of the world's great driving machines. Lighter, prettier, faster and closer to Porsche roots, the Speedster was an instant hit. It will always remain a Porsche icon and is extremely rare.

Low-cut soft top

The black soft top is designed to complement the lower windshield and is a real head hugger. When lowered, it occupies a space directly behind the driver and passenger (where the rear seats would normally be) that is covered with a hard plastic tonneau cover.

Winding windows

The original 356 Speedster has clip-on curtains in place of windows. The 911 Speedster has normal wind-down glass windows.

Club Sport seats

Because the roof line is so much lower, the seats are special—thin sporty buckets taken from the 911 Club Sport and mounted as low down in the floorpan as possible. This also makes it easier to get in and out.

Choice of Turbo-look body

Most Speedsters are fitted with a Turbo-style body kit, featuring wider wheel arches, front spoiler and skirts to mimic the great 911 Turbo; there are also wider tires to fill the big arches.

Rear-engined layout

The Speedster retains the classic Porsche layout of a rear-mounted flat-six engine with air cooling. This pushes the weight distribution severely to the rear, and while grip and traction are excellent, snap oversteer is a cornering trait of all 911s as a result.

Chopped-down windshield

Just like the 356 Speedster produced 25 years before it, the 911 Speedster has a severely lowered windshield that is also angled back by an additional five degrees. This reduces overall height by nearly two inches and gives the car a sportier look.

Lightweight

The effect of having a smaller glass area, a lighter soft top, Club Sport seats and no electric window or soft top motors gives a reduced overall weight. The Speedster is 150 lbs. lighter than the equivalent 911 Carrera convertible, giving it a slight performance edge.

Specifications

1989 Porsche 911 Speedster

ENGINE

Type: Horizontally-opposed six-cylinder

Construction: Aluminum block and heads

Valve gear: Two valves per cylinder operated by a single overhead camshaft per bank

Bore and stroke: 3.74 in. x 2.93 in.

Displacement: 3,164 cc

Compression ratio: 9.5:1

Induction system: Bosch fuel injection

Maximum power: 214 bhp at 5,900 rpm

Maximum torque: 195 lb-ft at 4,800 rpm

TRANSMISSION

Five-speed manual

BODY/CHASSIS

Monocoque two-door convertible

SPECIAL FEATURES

Supportive bucket seats hold the driver in place under hard cornering.

The small rear spoiler tucks in when not required at lower speeds.

RUNNING GEAR

Steering: Rack-and-pinion

Front suspension: MacPherson struts with longitudinal torsion bars, telescopic shock absorbers and anti-roll bar

Rear suspension: Semi-trailing arms with transverse torsion bars, telescopic shock absorbers and anti-roll bar

Brakes: Discs (front and rear)

Wheels: Alloy, 16-in. dia.

Tires: 205/55 16 (front), 225/50 16 (rear)

DIMENSIONS

Length: 168.9 in.   **Width:** 69.9 in.

Height: 50.4 in.   **Wheelbase:** 89.5 in.

Track: 56.4 in. (front), 58.7 in. (rear)

Weight: 2,925 lbs.

Porsche 959

In creating the 959, Porsche took the 911 design into the realms of fantasy. With quad cams and twin turbos it became a 190 mph racer that could tackle Le Mans, win the Paris-Dakar Rally and become the ultimate supercar.

"...thinly disguised racing car."

"As you approach the stunning 959, it's obvious why this is one of the most desired cars in recent history. Inside it's classic 911 taken to the next level. But the heavy racing clutch is the first sign of its true character—this is a thinly disguised racing car. Its four-wheel drive and powerful racing brakes give an added sense of security. At 4,500 rpm, civilized turns to savage. The second turbo kicks in, and you're howling past 60 mph in four seconds, hurtling toward a top speed of nearly 200 mph."

Despite its racing origins, the 959's interior is still luxurious with leather seats and full trim.

Milestones

1983 Porsche's new Group B car appears at the Frankfurt Motor Show. As well as being a street-legal supercar, Porsche intends to compete in the Group B class of international racing and rallying.

1984 Simplified 959s with 225 bhp, normally-aspirated engines run in the Paris-Dakar Rally. René Metge wins the event with Jacky Ickx taking sixth after an electrical fire.

959 won IMSA class at Le Mans.

1986 Metge and Jacky Ickx are first and second in the tough Paris-Dakar Raid with the rally version, and at Le Mans, the Racing 959 version finishes seventh overall and manages to win the IMSA class.

Earlier 959-type rally cars had four-wheel drive but no turbo and bore more resemblance to the 911.

1987 Production of the road cars gets under way with 250 built in 1987-88. Available in two versions: the Comfort with air conditioning, leather seats and electric windows; and the lighter and stripped-down Sport.

UNDER THE SKIN

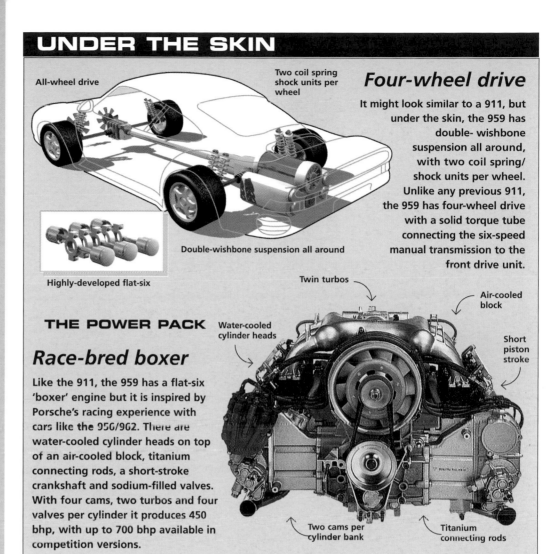

All-wheel drive

Two coil spring shock units per wheel

Highly-developed flat-six

Double-wishbone suspension all around

Four-wheel drive

It might look similar to a 911, but under the skin, the 959 has double-wishbone suspension all around, with two coil spring/shock units per wheel. Unlike any previous 911, the 959 has four-wheel drive with a solid torque tube connecting the six-speed manual transmission to the front drive unit.

THE POWER PACK

Race-bred boxer

Like the 911, the 959 has a flat-six 'boxer' engine but it is inspired by Porsche's racing experience with cars like the 956/962. There are water-cooled cylinder heads on top of an air-cooled block, titanium connecting rods, a short-stroke crankshaft and sodium-filled valves. With four cams, two turbos and four valves per cylinder it produces 450 bhp, with up to 700 bhp available in competition versions.

Twin turbos

Air-cooled block

Water-cooled cylinder heads

Short piston stroke

Two cams per cylinder bank

Titanium connecting rods

1986 Paris-Dakar car

The 959 was meant to be a winner in every form of racing and in 1986 the rally car, with René Metge driving, won the toughest rally of them all, the Paris-Dakar Raid. Another 959 driven by Jacky Ickx took second, while a third car finished sixth in the 959's final rally. The necessary 200 cars for homologation into Group B were not completed until 1988— after the Group B class was abandoned.

René Metge drove his 959 to victory on the Paris-Dakar Raid.

Porsche 959

Porsche deliberately made the 959 look as much like a 911 as possible—to help the 911's image and to show what the company had in store for their oldest and greatest model.

Front-mounted cooling system

The engine is in the rear but the radiator is at the front. The two side vents feed air to the twin engine oil coolers at the rear.

Adjustable shocks

The 959's eight shocks are adjustable to hard, medium or soft settings.

Rear wing

The rear wing helps generate the enormous downforce necessary to keep the 959 on the road at speeds over 190 mph.

Four-wheel drive

The 959 has four-wheel drive with six-speed gearbox and adjustable center and rear differentials. The normal torque split is slightly biased towards the rear wheels but varies according to wheel grip.

Double wishbone suspension

Double wishbone suspension is used all around, with two coil spring/shock units at each corner for extra wheel control.

Alloy and composite construction

Doors and hood are alloy and the other panels are a mix of fiberglass and Kevlar combining great strength and lightness.

Rear turbo vents

The twin turbos used on the 959 operate in sequence. The heat generated is expelled through these vents.

Porsche 911 rear lights

Despite the family resemblance, the only recognizable standard 911 production parts are the rear light clusters.

Variable ride height

At over 100 mph, the ride height was automatically lowered to 4.75 inches for increased stability. Over rough ground, the ride height could be increased to 6 or even 7 inches.

Specifications
1988 Porsche 959

ENGINE
Type: Flat-six
Construction: Alloy block and heads with alloy cylinder barrels and Nikasil coated bores
Valve gear: Four valves per cylinder operated by twin chain drive camshafts per bank of cylinders
Bore and stroke: 3.74 in. x 2.64 in.
Displacement: 2,851 cc
Compression ratio: 8.3:1
Induction system: Bosch Motronic fuel injection with twin intercooled KKK turbochargers
Maximum power: 450 bhp at 6,500 rpm
Maximum torque: 370 lb-ft at 5,500 rpm

TRANSMISSION
Type: Six-speed manual with four-wheel drive and adjustable center and rear diff.

BODY/CHASSIS
Alloy and composite paneled two-door, two-seat coupe with Porsche 911-based center monocoque section

SPECIAL FEATURES

Only one turbo operates below 4,500 rpm; above that the second engages, generating another 150 bhp.

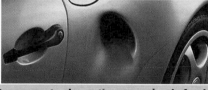

Large vents above the rear wheels feed air to the intercoolers for the twin turbochargers.

RUNNING GEAR
Steering: Rack-and-pinion
Front suspension: Twin wishbones with twin coil spring/shock units
Rear suspension: Twin wishbones with twin coil spring/shock units; electronic ride control
Brakes: Vented discs with ABS, 12.7 in. dia. (front), and 12 in. dia. (rear)
Wheels: Alloy 17 in.
Tires: 235/45 VR17 (front), 255/45 VR17 (rear)

DIMENSIONS
Length: 168 in.   **Width:** 72.5 in.
Height: 50.4 in.   **Wheelbase:** 89.5 in.
Track: 59.2 in. (front), 61 in. (rear)
Weight: 3,199 lbs.

Porsche BOXSTER

The first really new Porsche in 20 years, the Boxster uses the flat-six boxer engine that made it famous, but mounted in the middle of the car to give it incredible balance and handling.

"...the best-handling Porsche."

"For as good as the 911S and 928 are, the Boxster is still the best-handling car that Porsche has ever made. Its mid-engine design means it changes direction immediately at the touch of the incredibly precise steering, but it's not twitchy and quickly gives you total confidence. The ride, too, is excellent. It's comfortable without being soft, nor making the car seem vague. The engine is a gem, at least once it screams past 4,000 rpm as there's little low-down torque."

Much modernized interior still manages to retain traditional Porsche overtone—witness the array of overlapping instruments.

Milestones

1969 Porsche 914 is launched at the Frankfurt Motor Show. It is Porsche's first attempt at a mid-engined road car, but it uses the low-powered VW, 1.7-liter, flat-four engine of the VW 411. The more expensive 914/6 uses Porsche's own flat-six from the 911, which gives good performance including a top speed of 123 mph.

The 914's 'lowly' VW origins meant that it was never accepted as a true Porsche.

1972 Porsche-engined 914/6 is dropped in favor of a 2-liter, VW-engined version.

1971 Limited run of 20 916s is built. Using the 190-bhp, fuel-injected 911S engine, the car is axed before production officially begins.

1991 Chief Designer Harm Lagaay sets out to create a new two-seat roadster. The original concept is inspired by the 550 Spyder of the 1950s.

1993 Boxster concept car creates a sensation at every motor show it attends. Porsche promises to make the production car similar to the concept.

1996 Boxster goes into production. Porsche tries to keep up with the huge demand.

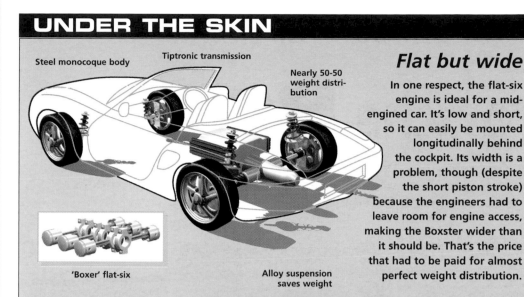

Steel monocoque body
Tiptronic transmission
Nearly 50-50 weight distribution
'Boxer' flat-six
Alloy suspension saves weight

Flat but wide

In one respect, the flat-six engine is ideal for a mid-engined car. It's low and short, so it can easily be mounted longitudinally behind the cockpit. Its width is a problem, though (despite the short piston stroke) because the engineers had to leave room for engine access, making the Boxster wider than it should be. That's the price that had to be paid for almost perfect weight distribution.

THE POWER PACK

Smaller flat-six

Although Porsche felt obliged to stick to the flat-six concept for the Boxster, they made the new engine water-cooled, which helps to reduce its noise output. At only 2,480 cc, it's smaller than any flat-six that's come from Porsche since the 911s of the early-1970s. It's of quad-cam design with four valves per cylinder and it's happiest when revved high for greater power. Its maximum power output of 204 bhp at 6,000 rpm is more impressive than the 181 lb-ft of torque at 4,500 rpm.

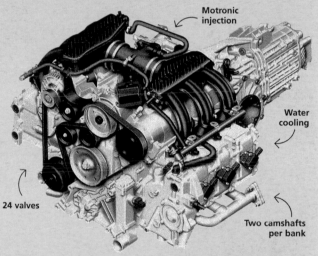

Motronic injection
Water cooling
24 valves
Two camshafts per bank

Show-stopper

Although substantially changed from the original concept car first revealed in 1993, and much simplified and rationalized for production, today's Boxster is still a heart-stoppingly beautiful exercise in mid-engined sports car styling.

The Boxster's handling is a perfect complement to that sweet engine.

Porsche BOXSTER

The Boxster achieves exactly what Porsche intended. It has even better handling than the previous 968 and it provides more driving pleasure while also being more affordable than the 911.

Automatic top

The power top on the Boxster unpacks and erects itself in just 12 seconds. When up, it's so rigid and secure it creates virtually no wind noise.

Water-cooled engine

With the engine right behind the cockpit, it would be difficult to duct enough air to it if it were a traditional air-cooled flat-six. Also, the lack of a sound-deadening water jacket means more noise. For these reasons, the Boxster engine is water cooled.

Unequal size tires

Standard wheels are 16 inches, but an optional package of 17-inch wheels is available. The rear tires are wider and the tire sizes are different front to back, with 205/50 ZR17s on the front and 255/45 ZR17s on the rear.

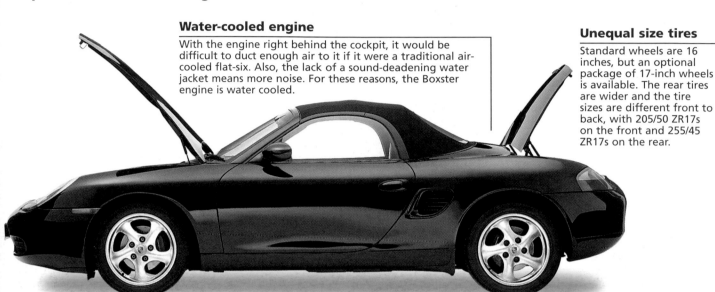

Smooth underbody

The underbody of the car has been made as smooth and uncluttered as possible, to minimize air turbulence underneath, making it less likely to affect the car's on-road behavior.

Strut suspension

Space restrictions mean struts are used all around. However, as the mid-engined Toyota MR2 showed in the early-1980s, excellent handling can still be achieved with these.

Optional Tiptronic transmission

Porsche expects that most people will want the manual five-speed transmission, but for those who like clutchless transmissions, the optional Tiptronic semi-automatic is now a five-speeder too.

Anti-buffeting screens

Mesh panels are incorporated into the twin roll-over hoops to shield occupants from high-speed wind-buffeting with the top down.

Alloy suspension arms

Porsche tried to save weight on the Boxster and the suspension arms are among the components made in alloy rather than steel.

Neutral weight distribution

The Boxster's weight distribution is a great improvement on the tail-heavy 911s, with a 48/52 front-to-rear split.

Unbeatable brakes

The tradition of superb Porsche brakes continues with the Boxster. Four-piston alloy calipers operate on big vented discs and, with the ABS, stop the Boxster from 60 mph in just 2.7 seconds, and from 100 mph in 4.3 seconds.

1997 Porsche Boxster

ENGINE
Type: Flat-six
Construction: Alloy block and heads
Valve gear: Four valves per cylinder operated by four overhead camshafts
Bore and stroke: 3.39 in. x 2.83 in.
Displacement: 2,480 cc
Compression ratio: 11.0:1
Induction system: Bosch Motronic electronic fuel injection
Maximum power: 204 bhp at 6,000 rpm
Maximum torque: 181 lb-ft at 4,500 rpm

TRANSMISSION
Five-speed manual

BODY/CHASSIS
Steel monocoque two-door, two-seat convertible

SPECIAL FEATURES

Mid-engined cars require cooling vents and intakes, which can be made into styling features.

Automatic top is the fastest in the business. It goes up in just 12 seconds.

RUNNING GEAR
Steering: Rack-and-pinion
Front suspension: MacPherson struts with longitudinal and transverse control arms and anti-roll bar
Rear suspension: MacPherson struts, longitudinal and transverse control arms and anti-roll bar
Brakes: Vented discs, 11.7 in. dia. (front), 11.5 in. dia. (rear)
Wheels: Alloy 7 in. x 17 in. (front), 9 in. x 17 in. (rear)
Tires: 205/50 ZR17 (front), 255/40 ZR17 (rear)

DIMENSIONS
Length: 169.9 in.   **Width:** 70.1 in.
Wheelbase: 95.1 in.   **Height:** 50.8 in.
Track: 57.3 in. (front), 59.4 in. (rear)
Weight: 2,756 lbs.

Renault SPORT SPIDER

Renault had never made an open two-seater sports car but really made up for lost time with the Spider. It's as fast as its outrageous looks suggest, has handling to match and even has its own race series.

"...race car for the road."

"The Spider really is a race car for the road with a bare interior and tachometer right in front of you. Like a racing car there are no rubber bushings in the suspension, giving instant response to any steering input. There's no trace of roll through turns yet the ride is still more than reasonable. It hits 30 mph in 2.6 seconds although you won't get below Renault's claim of seven seconds to 60 mph. But with such a good chassis, few of the world's sports cars can stay with it cross country."

To save weight the carpet, heater and in some countries, the windshield, are deleted.

Milestones

1995 Renault Sport Spider is one of the great surprises and star exhibits at the Geneva Motor Show. It is intended for a one-make endurance race series across Europe, but it is inevitable that there will be sufficient demand for a street version, despite the lack of a roof or, to begin with, even a windshield.

Spider's stunning looks are as big a selling point as its performance.

1996 As the Spider is only halfway practical in warm sunny climates, Renault unveils its solution for northern Europe at the Geneva Motor Show. The Spider is shown equipped with the optional windshield. Although a very rudimentary top is also available as an option to supplement the inferior standard tonneau cover, it's impractical at high speeds.

The Mégane Coupe's 16-valve engine is also used in the Sport Spider.

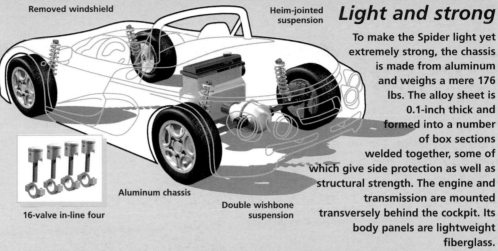

Removed windshield

Heim-jointed suspension

Aluminum chassis

16-valve in-line four

Double wishbone suspension

Light and strong

To make the Spider light yet extremely strong, the chassis is made from aluminum and weighs a mere 176 lbs. The alloy sheet is 0.1-inch thick and formed into a number of box sections welded together, some of which give side protection as well as structural strength. The engine and transmission are mounted transversely behind the cockpit. Its body panels are lightweight fiberglass.

THE POWER PACK

Williams Renault

The Spider's fuel-injected 2-liter four has been seen before, in the Clio Williams and then the current Mégane 16-valve Coupe. It produces 150 bhp thanks to its twin camshafts, fuel injection, and 16-valve layout, which also allows the engine to rev with real enthusiasm. Peak power is produced at 6,000 rpm. Its long stroke, however, also helps give it an impressive maximum torque output of 140 lb-ft at 4,500 rpm. The car's excellent chassis, though, is capable of handling much more power.

Twin camshafts

Alloy cylinder head

Four valves per cylinder

Iron block

Renault racer

The racing version of the Sport Spider that is built to compete in the Elf Renault Sport Spider Cup has no windshield, a six-speed transmission, wider wheels and tires, a lower ride height, a brake balance adjustment, stiff suspension and a roll cage for safety.

Renault Sport Spider Cup allows owners to get the most from their Spiders.

Renault SPORT SPIDER ▐▐

Despite huge success in Formula One racing, Renault needed a street car to show its racing heritage. One answer was the Sport Spider, a state-of-the-art sports car that is fast, advanced and equally at home on the road or track.

Advanced suspension

Renault discarded conventional rubber bushes and used bushless ball joints in the suspension, along with pushrods to operate the inboard coil springs.

Recaro seats

Because the Spider can generate high cornering loads, it uses Recaro seats that give good lateral support.

Mid-mounted engine

The Spider uses the 2-liter 16-valve twin cam engine fitted to the Mégane Coupe. It's mid-mounted for perfect front-to-rear weight balance.

Alloy chassis

The Spider's strength comes from light alloy chassis members made of extruded aluminum which has 1.5 times the energy absorbing capacity of steel on impact.

Alpine components

Renault made use of its experience in building the Alpine A610 supercar, giving the Spider its hubs, brake discs and calipers.

Adjustable pedal box

Although the seats move, the pedal box can also be adjusted in or out just as easily by up to 4.9 inches.

Digital speedometer

A digital readout in the center of the dashboard gives the car's speed. The main conventional analog dial right in front of the driver is the tach, just as it would be in a racing car.

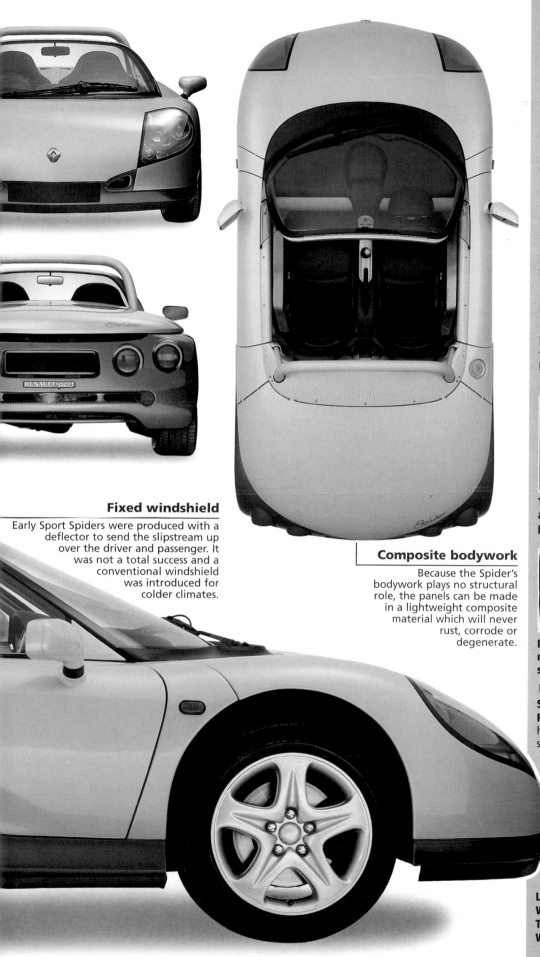

Fixed windshield

Early Sport Spiders were produced with a deflector to send the slipstream up over the driver and passenger. It was not a total success and a conventional windshield was introduced for colder climates.

Composite bodywork

Because the Spider's bodywork plays no structural role, the panels can be made in a lightweight composite material which will never rust, corrode or degenerate.

Specifications
1997 Renault Sport Spider

ENGINE
Type: In-line four
Construction: Cast-iron block and light alloy cylinder head
Valve gear: Four valves per cylinder operated by twin overhead camshafts
Bore and stroke: 3.25 in. x 3.66 in.
Displacement: 1,998 cc
Compression ratio: 9.8:1
Induction system: Electronic fuel injection
Maximum power: 150 bhp at 6,000 rpm
Maximum torque: 140 lb-ft at 4,500 rpm

TRANSMISSION
Five-speed manual

BODY/CHASSIS
Extruded and welded alloy frame with fiberglass, two-door, two-seat convertible body

SPECIAL FEATURES

The aluminum chassis is extremely light, at only 176 lbs. This helps give excellent performance from the 16-valve engine.

Renault put the big circular tachometer right ahead of the driver, with a digital speedometer off to the side.

RUNNING GEAR
Steering: Rack-and-pinion
Front suspension: Double wishbones with horizontally mounted inboard coil spring/shocks and anti-roll bar
Rear suspension: Double wishbones with longitudinally mounted coil/spring shocks and anti-roll bar
Brakes: Vented discs, 11.8 in. dia. (front and rear)
Wheels: Alloy 8 in. x 16 in. (front), 9 in. x 16 in. (rear)
Tires: 205/60 VR16 (front), 225/50 VR16 (rear)

DIMENSIONS
Length: 149.4 in.   **Width:** 72 in.
Wheelbase: 92.2 in.   **Height:** 49.2 in.
Track: 60.7 in. (front), 60.5 in. (rear)
Weight: 2,106 lbs.

Toyota MR2

In the 1980s, Toyota built the best small, mid-engined, mass-production sports car in the world. For the '90s, they made the engine bigger and more powerful, and gave the car a new, smooth, rounded body to go with it.

"...wonderful balance."

"The MR2 is no longer the incredibly nimble sports car it was when it was born. It's grown bigger, heavier and more civilized. Unlike the old car, you don't need to worry about taking the modern MR2 right to the limit on a twisty road. It won't spin unless you do something really stupid. It gives you the confidence to use all of its impressive mid-engined capabilities of wonderful balance and amazing cornering. With the revised twin-cam and 173 bhp, it has the power to exploit that chassis. You must rev hard to find the power, but it doesn't complain—and that's all part of the enjoyment."

With irrepressibly Japanese styling throughout, the cabin is durable and well placed.

Milestones

1984 MR2 introduced with a 1.6-liter, twin-cam engine.

1986 T-bar roof with removable glass roof panels is added to the series.

The first-generation MR2 proved to be very popular.

1986 Supercharger installed on some models to increase power and performance.

1989 New-generation MR2 is launched with a larger, 2-liter, twin-cam engine producing 158 bhp. It is wider, longer and much heavier—yet it is lower and sleeker.

Refinement and build quality improved with the second-generation MR2.

1994 Engine revisions increase power by 15 bhp. Torque output stays the same and suspension adjustments make it easier and safer for the average driver.

UNDER THE SKIN

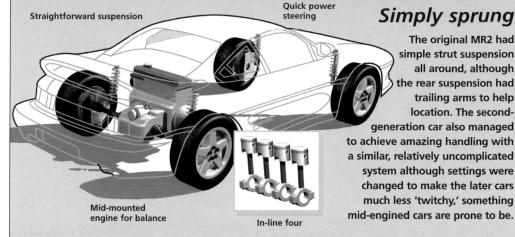

Straightforward suspension

Quick power steering

Mid-mounted engine for balance

In-line four

Simply sprung

The original MR2 had simple strut suspension all around, although the rear suspension had trailing arms to help location. The second-generation car also managed to achieve amazing handling with a similar, relatively uncomplicated system although settings were changed to make the later cars much less 'twitchy,' something mid-engined cars are prone to be.

THE POWER PACK

Willing and able

Nobody extracts more from a non-turbo 2-liter engine than Toyota. Helped by its twin camshafts, 16 valves and variable induction system, the iron-block 'square' (3.39 in. bore and stroke) engine produces an outstanding (for its size) 173 bhp, and it's quite happy to rev sweetly to the heady 7,000 rpm where that peak power is produced. Torque output is much less and produced fairly high at 4,800 rpm, but with such a free-revving engine, it hardly matters. High power is unusually matched to a fine reputation for reliability.

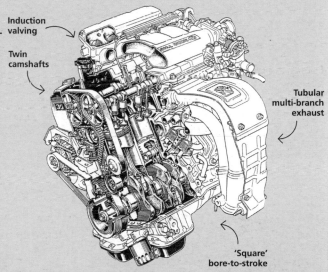

Induction valving

Twin camshafts

Tubular multi-branch exhaust

'Square' bore-to-stroke

Classic status?

Although they only have 1.6-liter engines and 122 bhp, the first MR2s are only slightly slower than the later bigger cars and are even more agile. Although they were easier to spin, they were more fun to drive and are now becoming accepted as classics.

More delicate-looking than muscular, the original MR2 still cut the mustard.

Toyota MR2

As civilized as any conventional Japanese coupe, the MR2 offers the handling balance that only mid-engined cars can really achieve. It has the speed and performance to make that balance worthwhile.

Side-impact beams

The move to increase safety affects all new cars, the MR2 included. It now has side-impact bars to limit intrusion when the car is struck side-on.

Mid-engined

Other than Acura's NSX and Honda's Civic Del Sol, Toyota is the only Japanese manufacturer to mass-produce a mid-engined car. The four-cylinder engine is mounted transversely behind the cabin.

Strut suspension

With the MR2, Toyota proves that you don't need the complication of the latest multi-link suspension or a classic double-wishbone design to give wonderful handling. Toyota achieves that with struts front and rear.

MR2 name

There's a simple explanation for the MR2 name. It stands for Mid-engine, Rear-drive, 2-seater.

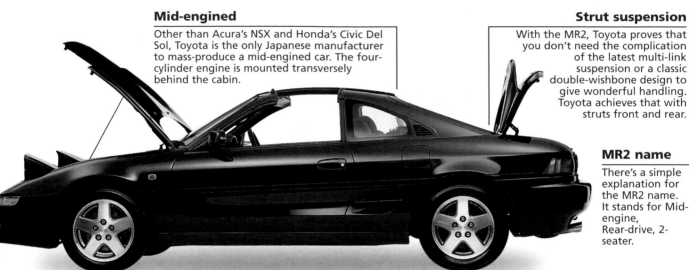

Power-assisted steering

Yet another change from the first- to second-generation MR2 is the inclusion of power-assisted steering, even though there's relatively little weight over the front wheels in a mid-engined car.

Rear weight distribution

Surprisingly, the mid-engine location does not give the MR2 perfect weight distribution. It's split 42/58 front to rear.

Larger rear tires

The first-generation MR2 runs on the same size tires all around. For the bigger, second-generation car, Toyota installed larger rear tires to give the back end more grip.

Rear spoiler

Even though both generations of MR2 have been rear-heavy, a rear spoiler designed to increase downforce on the driven wheels has always been a feature of the car.

ABS

The first MR2s did not have ABS, but because the car has moved upmarket and become more expensive, ABS has been standard since 1994.

Specifications
1997 Toyota MR2

ENGINE
Type: In-line four cylinder
Construction: Cast-iron block and alloy head
Valve gear: Four valves per cylinder operated by twin overhead camshafts
Bore and stroke: 3.39 in. x 3.39 in.
Displacement: 1,998 cc
Compression ratio: 10.3:1
Induction system: Electronic fuel injection
Maximum power: 173 bhp at 7,000 rpm
Maximum torque: 137 lb-ft at 4,800 rpm

TRANSMISSION
Five-speed manual

BODY/CHASSIS
Steel monocoque with two-door coupe body

SPECIAL FEATURES

T-bar roof design provides near-convertible motoring pleasure, but helps keep the body rigid.

It's certainly a stylish addition to the MR2's rounded lines, but at speed, the rear spoiler aids in stability.

RUNNING GEAR
Steering: Rack-and-pinion
Front suspension: MacPherson struts with anti-roll bar
Rear suspension: MacPherson struts with trailing arms and anti-roll bar
Brakes: Discs, vented 10.8 in. dia. (front), solid 11.1 in. dia. (rear). ABS
Wheels: Alloy, 6 in. x 15 in.
Tires: 195/55 VR15 (front), 225/50 VR15 (rear)

DIMENSIONS
Length: 164.2 in. **Width:** 66.9 in.
Height: 48.6 in. **Wheelbase:** 48.6 in.
Track: 57.9 in. (front), 57.1 in. (rear)
Weight: 2,833 lbs.

Toyota SUPRA

With the 1993 model, Toyota moved the Supra from an overweight and ugly cruiser to an affordable and dramatically styled junior supercar capable of more than 155 mph thanks to its 326-bhp twin-turbo, twin-cam engine.

"...Be prepared for excitement."

"On looks alone, the Supra has a very extroverted styling. When you slide behind the wheel and stomp the accelerator to the floor, be prepared for excitement. Off idle, the whistling under the hood indicates that the first turbocharger is spooling up. At 4,000 rpm both turbos are now forcing air into the Supra's 2,997 cc engine. The engine is tuned for mid- to high-end power, but because of a governor, can only get the car up to 156 mph. Without it the Supra would easily hit 180 mph."

The luxurious interior of the twin-turbo Supra really gave Nissan, Mazda and Porsche something to worry about.

Milestones

1984 The six-cylinder
Supra line begins with a 2.8-liter car with the crisp, sharp-edged styling similar to that used on the contemporary Celica. The car is normally aspirated and not very impressive. The Supra reaches 60 mph in 7.9 seconds and has a top speed of 125 mph.

The Supra was the first Toyota six-cylinder sports car since the exotic 2000GT.

1986 Supra gets a
facelift with a much more rounded shape and a power output increased to 201 bhp, giving a top speed of 135 mph.

The second-generation Supra was fast, but not as competent as the current model.

1989 Hinting at the
way Toyota was going to go, the Supra is given more power with a turbocharged version of the straight-six engine that produces 232 bhp.

1993 The current
Supra is introduced two years later than planned. Extra time was needed to build a car to outperform the Nissan 300ZX. It is more powerful, lighter and faster than the previous model.

UNDER THE SKIN

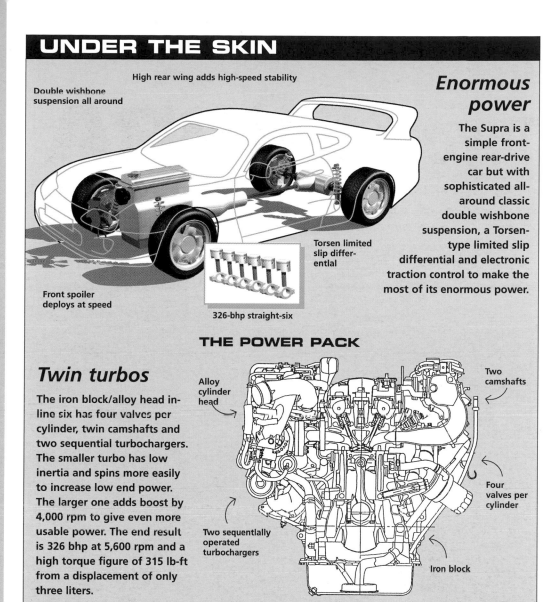

High rear wing adds high-speed stability

Double wishbone suspension all around

Front spoiler deploys at speed

Torsen limited slip differential

326-bhp straight-six

Enormous power

The Supra is a simple front-engine rear-drive car but with sophisticated all-around classic double wishbone suspension, a Torsen-type limited slip differential and electronic traction control to make the most of its enormous power.

THE POWER PACK

Twin turbos

The iron block/alloy head in-line six has four valves per cylinder, twin camshafts and two sequential turbochargers. The smaller turbo has low inertia and spins more easily to increase low end power. The larger one adds boost by 4,000 rpm to give even more usable power. The end result is 326 bhp at 5,600 rpm and a high torque figure of 315 lb-ft from a displacement of only three liters.

Alloy cylinder head

Two camshafts

Four valves per cylinder

Two sequentially operated turbochargers

Iron block

Flashy and fast

Some critics find the Supra too flashy, but they should take another look beyond the tall wing and massive hood and side scoops. It's hard to fault the Supra's lines, as it looks good from any angle and it is given real presence by those large-diameter wheels.

The flashy Supra has all the power to match its extraordinary looks.

Toyota **SUPRA**

The previous Supra was quick but bland, clumsy looking and clumsy to drive—the current sports car, however, is in another class. Stunning looks and that high rear wing promise high performance, and that's exactly what the Supra delivers.

Traction control

Using the ABS sensors, traction control works by lightly applying the rear brakes, reducing fuel supply and retarding ignition just enough to stop the rear wheels from spinning.

Six-speed transmission

Like the Porsche 968, the Supra uses the tough Getrag six-speed transmission. However, the turbocharged engine isn't peaky and does not need constant gear shifting to get the best from it.

Tall rear wing

The huge wing helps the Supra remain stable at the high speeds it can easily reach.

G-sensing ABS

The Supra ABS anti-lock braking system has a g-force sensor so the brakes are modulated through corners to stop the brakes from locking and the car sliding.

Extending front spoiler

If the Supra travels above 56 mph for more than five seconds, the front spoiler automatically deploys to increase front downforce.

Twin wishbone suspension

Classic racing-style double-wishbone suspension is used in the front and rear to give excellent wheel location and precise handling.

Ultra low-profile tires

As the wishbone suspension allows virtually no change in camber, the Supra can run on very low-profile tires which are always 'square' on the road.

Twin turbochargers

The first, smaller turbo helps low-down performance before the bigger one kicks in at higher rpm. Both are intercooled.

Torsen differential

The Torsen-type limited slip differential is a mechanical device using worm gears (rather than fluid as in a viscous coupling) to distribute torque between the rear wheels.

Specifications
1996 Toyota Supra

ENGINE
Type: Straight-six twin-cam
Construction: Cast-iron block and alloy cylinder head
Valve gear: Four valves per cylinder operated by twin overhead cams
Bore and stroke: 3.39 in. x 3.39 in.
Displacement: 2,997 cc
Induction system: Electronic fuel injection with twin sequential turbochargers
Maximum power: 326 bhp at 5,600 rpm
Maximum torque: 315 lb-ft at 4,800 rpm

TRANSMISSION
Six-speed manual or four-speed automatic

BODY/CHASSIS
Steel monocoque two-door 2+2 coupe

SPECIAL FEATURES

The Supra receives stability at high speeds thanks to this enormous wing.

Sequential turbos give the Supra its power—one operates at lower rpm for improved torque, the other comes on by 4,000 rpm for high-end power.

RUNNING GEAR
Steering: Rack-and-pinion
Front suspension: Twin wishbones with coil springs, telescopic shock absorbers and anti-roll bar
Rear suspension: Twin wishbones with coil springs, telescopic shock absorbers and anti-roll bar
Brakes: Four-wheel vented discs, 12.6 in. dia. with ABS
Wheels/tires: Alloy 8 in. x 17 in. (front), 9.5 in. x 17 in. (rear) with 235/45 ZR17 (front) and 255/40 ZR17 (rear) tires

DIMENSIONS
Length: 177.8 in. **Width:** 71.3 in.
Wheelbase: 100.4 in. **Height:** 49.8 in.
Track: 59.8 in. (front), 60 in. (rear)
Weight: 3,445 lbs.

TVR **GRIFFITH**

The Griffith is a world away from TVR's kit-car origins. The quality is high, the design outstanding and the performance from its latest 5-liter V8 engine nothing short of staggering.

"...guarantees excitement."

"More than 300 bhp in a light car that has a short wheelbase guarantees excitement and the Griffith delivers a huge amount of it. Lurid power is only a touch of the throttle away, as the power overcomes the grip of the big rear tires despite the limited slip differential. Before the power-assisted steering became available, it took an acute combination of strength and finesse to control such behavior. You also need a firm hand for the gear shifter and a strong leg for the clutch, but the Griffith's breathtaking acceleration makes it all worth the effort."

Smart and stylish dashboard of the Griffith uses many recognizable switches and gauges.

Milestones

1963 The distant ancestor of
the current Griffith has a Ford V8 and is named after U.S. Ford dealer Jack Griffith. It can reach 160 mph, but the car is very difficult to drive fast.

By the late 1980s, the wedge-shaped TVRs were beginning to look dated.

1990 TVR builds another Griffith,
as a show car for the British Motor Show. Reaction is enthusiastic, so TVR decides to put the Griffith into production.

The Racing Tuscan showed TVR's potential.

1992 The production Griffith debuts.
It is designed to use a variety of Rover V8 engines, from a 'basic' 240-bhp version, through a 250-bhp stage and up to the 280-bhp 4.3-liter version.

1993 An even more powerful
Griffith appears. The engine is enlarged to 5 liters, to form the 340-bhp Griffith 500.

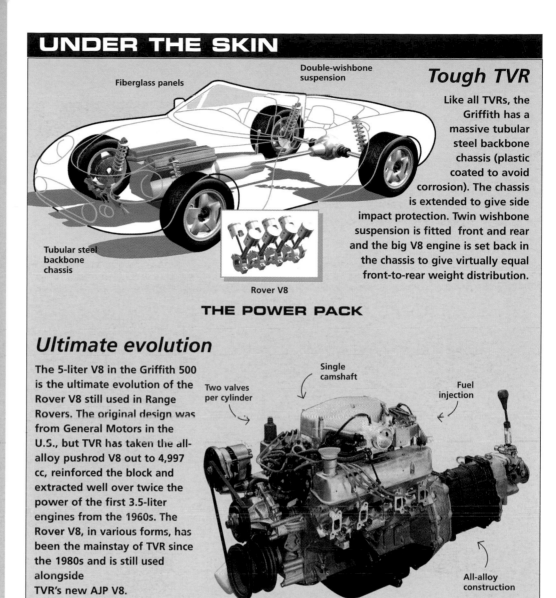

Fiberglass panels

Double-wishbone suspension

Tubular steel backbone chassis

Rover V8

Tough TVR

Like all TVRs, the Griffith has a massive tubular steel backbone chassis (plastic coated to avoid corrosion). The chassis is extended to give side impact protection. Twin wishbone suspension is fitted front and rear and the big V8 engine is set back in the chassis to give virtually equal front-to-rear weight distribution.

THE POWER PACK

Ultimate evolution

The 5-liter V8 in the Griffith 500 is the ultimate evolution of the Rover V8 still used in Range Rovers. The original design was from General Motors in the U.S., but TVR has taken the all-alloy pushrod V8 out to 4,997 cc, reinforced the block and extracted well over twice the power of the first 3.5-liter engines from the 1960s. The Rover V8, in various forms, has been the mainstay of TVR since the 1980s and is still used alongside TVR's new AJP V8.

Single camshaft

Two valves per cylinder

Fuel injection

All-alloy construction

Best of British

The Griffith's stunning looks don't come from an expensive Italian styling house or from computer-aided design, but from the eye of TVR boss Peter Wheeler and engineer John Ravenscroft. They sculpted a full-size foam model until they arrived at the Griffith's stunning shape.

Designed in-house, the Griffith looks spectacular from any angle.

TVR GRIFFITH

The Griffith is just like a modern-day AC Cobra, the concept being a very large powerful engine in a small convertible. Like the Cobra, there's very little to rival the Griffith.

Fiberglass bodywork

The fiberglass body is bolted to the tubular steel chassis to make a stronger, stiffer overall structure.

Flat-mounted radiator

The radiator is mounted at a very shallow angle and the air is drawn through it by twin electric fans. There was room to allow this because the engine is set so far back.

Rover transmission

Sensibly, the TVR use the same tough, five-speed transmission that Rover used in the fastest of its V8-engined cars, the Vitesse.

Tubular steel chassis

The tubular steel chassis is designed to give the Griffith an extremely strong central backbone, which is the way TVR has always designed its chassis.

Larger rear wheels

To cope with its huge power output, the Griffith has larger, 7.5 inch x 16 inch OZ Racing split-rim alloy rear wheels.

Optional leather trim

If you want your Griffith to be luxurious as well as very fast then leather seats and trim are an option.

Equal weight distribution

With the engine set well back in the chassis, the heavy Rover transmission is near the center of the car: The weight distribution is almost ideal at 51 percent front, 49 percent rear.

Wishbone suspension

Twin wishbone suspension is used all around on the Griffith. The rear suspension is very similar to that found on the mighty TVR Tuscan racers.

Ford Sierra final drive

The final drive housing is actually a Ford Sierra part, but the gears inside are much stronger, with a Quaife limited slip differential to reduce wheelspin and help traction.

Specifications
1993 TVR Griffith 500

ENGINE
Type: V8, overhead valve
Construction: Alloy block and heads
Valve gear: Two valves per cylinder operated by single block-mounted camshaft via pushrods and rockers
Bore and stroke: 3.54 in. x 3.54 in.
Displacement: 4,997 cc
Compression ratio: 10:1
Induction system: Electronic fuel injection
Maximum power: 340 bhp at 5,500 rpm
Maximum torque: 351 lb-ft at 4,000 rpm

TRANSMISSION
Five-speed manual

BODY/CHASSIS
Fiberglass two-door, two-seat convertible with tubular steel backbone chassis

SPECIAL FEATURES

The V8 has massive exhaust headers which have to be routed around the front of the engine.

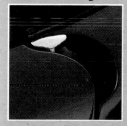

Small door handles are neatly recessed so the lines of the car are not spoiled.

RUNNING GEAR
Steering: Rack-and-pinion
Front suspension: Twin wishbones, coil springs, telescopic shocks and anti-roll bar
Rear suspension: Twin wishbones, coil springs and telescopic shocks
Brakes: Disc, vented 10.2 in. dia. (front), solid 10.7 in. dia. (rear)
Wheels: Alloy OZ, 7 in. x 15 in. (front), 7.5 in. x 16 in. (rear)
Tires: 215/50ZR15 (front), 225/50ZR16 (rear)

DIMENSIONS
Length: 156.1 in.   **Width:** 76.5 in.
Wheelbase: 58.4 in.   **Height:** 46.7 in.
Track: 58 in. (front), 58.4 in. (rear)
Weight: 2,304 lbs.

Index

100, Austin-Healey 25
100/6, Austin-Healey 25
240Z, Datsun 48–51
260Z, Datsun 49
275 GTB, Ferrari 73
280Z, Datsun 49
300SL, Mercedes-Benz
  148–51
328, BMW 33
356, Porsche 160–3
507, BMW 33
911 Speedster, Porsche 164–7
914, Porsche 173
916, Porsche 173
959, Porsche 168–71
3000, Austin-Healey 24–7
Acura NSX, Honda 92–5
Alfa Romeo
  Giulietta SS 13
  Giulietta SZ 12–15
  Proteo 9
  Spider 8–11
  SZ 9
Artioli, Romano 36, 37
Aston Martin
  DB6 17
  DB7 16–19
  DBS 17
  Vantage 20–3
  Virage 21
Austin-Healey
  100 25
  100/6 25
  3000 24–7

Bertone 13, 117
BMW
  328 33
  507 33
  M1 28–31
  Z1 33
  Z3 32–5
Boxer, Ferrari 68–71
Boxster, Porsche 172–5
Bracq, Paul 29
Bugatti, EB110 36–9

C7R, Callaway 45
Callaway
  C7R 45
  Corvette 45
Callaway, Reeves 21
Camaro Z28, Chevrolet 40–3
Chevrolet

Camaro Z28 40–3
  Corvette 44–7
Corvette, Chevrolet 44–7
Cosmo, Mazda 141
Countach, Lamborghini 7,
  104–7
Craft, Chris 121

Datsun
  240Z 48–51
  260Z 49
  280Z 49
  Z432 49
Daytona, Ferrari 72–5
DB6, Aston Martin 17
DB7, Aston Martin 16–19
DBS, Aston Martin 17
De Tomaso
  Mangusta 53
  Pantera 52–5
DeLorean, John 57
DeLorean, DMC 56–9
Diablo, Lamborghini 108–11
Dino, Ferrari 76–9
DMC, DeLorean 56–9
Dodge, Viper 60–3

E-type, Jaguar 6, 96–9
EB110, Bugatti 36–9
Elise, Lotus 124–7
Esprit V8, Lotus 128–31

F1, McLaren 144–7
F355, Ferrari 64–7
Ferrari
  275 GTB 73
  512 F1 81
  Boxer 68–71
  Daytona 72–5
  Dino 76–9
  F355 64–7
  Testarossa 69, 80–3
Ford
  GT40 84–7
  Mustang GT 88–91
  Pantera 53

Gandini, Marcello 113
Ghibli, Maserati 132–5
Giulietta SS, Alfa Romeo 13
Giulietta SZ, Alfa Romeo
  12–15
Griffith, TVR 188–91
GT40, Ford 84–7

Honda, Acura NSX 92–5

Ickx, Jacky 169

Jaguar
  E-type 6, 96–9
  XJS 101
  XK8 100–3

Koenig, Will 109

Lamborghini
  Countach 7, 104–7
  Diablo 108–11
  Miura 112–15
Lancia, Stratos 116–19
Le Mans
  Ferrari Boxer at 69
  Ford GT40 at 85
  Honda Acura NSX at 93
  Maclaren F1 at 145
  Porsche 959 at 169
Light Car Company, Rocket
  120–3
Lotus
  Elise 124–7
  Esprit V8 128–31

M1, BMW 28–31
M Roadster, BMW 33
McLaren, F1 144–7
Mangusta, De Tomaso 53
Maserati
  Ghibli 132–5
  Shamal 133
Mazda
  Cosmo 141
  Miata 136–9
  RX-7 140–3
Mégane, Renault 177
Mercedes-Benz, 300SL
  148–51
Metge, René 169
MGB 152–5
Miata, Mazda 136–9
Miura, Lamborghini 112–15
MR2, Toyota 180–3
Murray, Gordon 121
Mustang GT, Ford 88–91

Novaro, Emile 109
NSX, Honda Acura 92–5

O'Rourke, Steve 69

Panoz, Danny 157
Panoz, Roadster 156–9
Pantera, De Tomaso 52–5
Paris-Dakar Raid 169
Pininfarina 77, 81, 101
Porsche
  356 160–3
  911 Speedster 164–7
  914 173
  916 173
  959 168–71
  Boxster 172–5
Proteo, Alfa Romeo 9

Renault
  Mégane 177
  Sport Spider 176–9
Roadster
  BMW 33
  Panoz 156–9
Rocket, Light Car Company
  120–3
RX-7, Mazda 140–3

Shamal, Maserati 133
Speedster
  Porsche 356 161
  Porsche 911 164–7
Spider, Alfa Romeo 8–11
Sport Spider, Renault 176–9
Stratos, Lancia 116–19
Supra, Toyota 184–7
SZ, Alfa Romeo 9

Testarossa, Ferrari 69, 80–3
Toyota
  MR2 180–3
  Supra 184–7
TVR, Griffith 188–91

Vantage, Aston Martin 20–3
Viper, Dodge 60–3
Virage, Aston Martin 21

XJS, Jaguar 101
XK8, Jaguar 100–3

Z1, BMW 33
Z3, BMW 32–5
Z432, Datsun 49
Zagato 13